BUCKAROO

Visions and Voices of the American Cowboy

Edited by Hal Cannon and Thomas West

CALLAWAY

SIMON & SCHUSTER

New York · London · Toronto · Sydney · Tokyo · Singapore

SIMON & SCHUSTER
Simon & Schuster Building, Rockefeller Center
1230 Avenue of the Americas
New York, New York 10020

Don Edwards and Waddie Mitchell appear by courtesy of Warner Bros. Records, Inc.
R.W. Hampton appears by courtesy of Adobe Records.
Buck Ramsey appears by courtesy of Fiel Publications, Inc.
Riders in the Sky appear by courtesy of Columbia Records.
Ian Tyson appears by courtesy of Vanguard Records.

Photographs © 1993 William Albert Allard, Peter de Lory, Jay Dusard, Bank Langmore,
Kurt Markus, Norman Mauskopf, Martin Schreiber, and National Geographic Society (p. 43).
Watercolor paintings © 1993 William Matthews.

Peter de Lory, Jay Dusard, and Norman Mauskopf
are represented by the Swanstock Photographic Agency.

10 9 8 7 6 5 4 3 2 1

Library of Congress Cataloging-in-Publication Data
p.   cm.
ISBN: 0-671-88054-3 : $45.00
1. Cowboys—West (U.S.) 2. Cowboys — Poetry.
3. Cowboys — Songs and music. 4. Folk songs, English — West (U.S.)
F596.B89 1993
978 — DC20   93-26594
CIP

HALF-TITLE PAGE: Montana, watercolor by William Matthews
FRONTISPIECE: The Spanish Ranch, Tuscarora, Nevada, photograph by Kurt Markus
TITLE PAGE: Rick Bates, YP Ranch, Tuscarora, Nevada, photograph by Kurt Markus

CONTENTS

CD TRACK *17, Home on the Range,* is sung by Riders in the Sky

FOREWORD · VISIONS AND VOICES

In January of 1985 I stood with buckaroo Waddie Mitchell in back of two hundred chairs we had just set up for the first Cowboy Poetry Gathering in Elko, Nevada. Waddie looked at me. "We should put some of these chairs away," he said, "this is going to be embarrassing."

I thought back to the thousands of back-road miles my folklorist friends and I had driven to ranches asking for recitations; the letters to editors of a thousand rural Western papers requesting ranch poets to step forward; the many ranch scrapbooks I had leafed through, filled with photographs of prize bulls framed lovingly next to snapshots of children dressed in stiff Levi's with eight-inch folded cuffs going off to school for the first time, and poems by Bruce Kiskaddon cut out from the livestock auction calendar. Who was this Kiskaddon? Why did the bull and the kids' faces change but the poems by Kiskaddon endure?

Just then, ranchers and cowboy families started filling the chairs. We organizers stood back, amazed, at the fifteen hundred people who entered the auditorium, having traveled in the middle of winter, to the middle of nowhere, for a poetry reading. These people had convened to recite their own poems, to tell their own stories, and to sing their own songs.

It has always seemed curious that one occupation, that of the cowboy, is so charged with mythic qualities. There is such a wealth of expressions — written and spoken, sketched and painted, braided and sewn — associated with this relatively uncommon occupation that one wonders if it only has to do with cattleherding. There are no historic narratives from the original cowboy days, the trail drives following the Civil War, which adequately explain the chemistry that brought an incredibly diverse lot of men together, in the wilderness, and forced them to rely on each other and their animals during long and trying odysseys. From this experience came an astonishing amalgam of life that would identify Americans forever. It was a jazz of Irish storytelling, Scottish seafaring and cattle tending, Moorish and Spanish horsemanship, European cavalry traditions, African improvisation, and Native American experience, if also oppression. All the old ingredients can be heard and seen in the cowboying way of life even today.

By the 1880s, books of cowboy poems began to appear, and cowboy novels spread like prairie fire. Around 1910 cowboy songs were being collected. By then, the cowboy image was set on its own course, a course that would inspire the music, films, and literature that, as the years passed, would stray increasingly from the reality of ranch life.

By the early 1980s, when our concerted effort to document cowboy poetry and music began, the commercial cowboy fire had burned out, and the ranching community was adamantly suspicious of any and all interpretations of their culture by outsiders. At the same time, most ranch people were shy in presenting their story to a larger world. The art of the ranching community was an insider's affair.

This is no longer the case. A true renaissance of cowboy arts is under way. It is largely powered by the pressure the modern world exerts on a way of life that is foreign to it. Open-land grazing, one hallmark of the West, is being challenged by grasping urban centers, by recreationalists, and by environmentalists. The economic viability of all but a few rural Western towns is under threat. Beyond being just a cry from the wilderness, or providing us with a mere nostalgic look at a vanishing past, cowboy poetry, story, and song possess a strength and knowledge that are worthy of everyone's attention.

Although cowboy poetry is thought of as a male tradition, some of the most powerful stories being told today are by women. Cowboy writers are not easily stereotyped. The men and women who have chosen to express themselves using their ranching experience are a diverse group. Some are educated at the best schools in America; some are veterans and patriots; some consider themselves throw-backs to another age; some are modern. They represent every generation.

Today there are more than one hundred fifty poetry gatherings in small Western towns. More than five hundred books of ranch poetry have been published in the past century as well as a handful of journals and magazines that printed the poetry. There is a revitalized cowboy singing tradition, and cowboy craft is doing better than ever.

What does this mean to Americans today, most of whom may question the very existence of the cowboy? To find pertinence, one needs to park the John Wayne imitation, slip off the pointy snakeskin boots . . . and open up the eyes. The cowboy in this book has nothing hackneyed about him. He has nothing to do with the cowboy Europeans invoke when talking of American politicians and business-men who act with little regard for others. The cow-boy of this book is what Nevada rancher Jack Walther prefers to call the "buckaroo," a person of innate nobility who maintains pride about work that probably gives the poorest pay and demands the highest skill of any job in America.

True, ranch traditions are themselves super-charged with the popular cowboy image, but with that image comes a legacy of vision and courage. The cowboy social traditions are basically old-style rural values that place a premium on good neighboring and a conservatism born of nature, not of ignorance. Ranch people are grounded in a literal sense, whereas most people have lost their day-to-day reliance on living outside and being tied to what the earth can provide. This ancient relationship with nature has disappeared from most of our lives. In the cramped conditions of city living we have lost contact with animal intelligence. In open places people still live with animals, they live with wildness. Since the trail drive days, cowboys have placed a special value on language and stories to instruct and entertain during seasons of hard work and spartan existence. Cow-boys respect tradition, but they also innovate within the tradition, not feeling obliged to uphold all the institutions and conventions that we are addicted to in the city.

The stories, songs, and poems of the new cow-boy movement honestly recognize loss. They protest the modern world and offer advice to a society that risks being overtaken by less than human values. They make us laugh with the ridiculous. They span the human experience of life and livelihood on the ranch. Insiders will appreciate this material best. But the reason this book and recording are being offered to a larger public is that we believe there are visions and voices here which can enlighten us all.

Hal Cannon
Western Folklife Center, Elko, Nevada

OVERLEAF: ZX Ranch, Paisley, Oregon, photograph by Kurt Markus

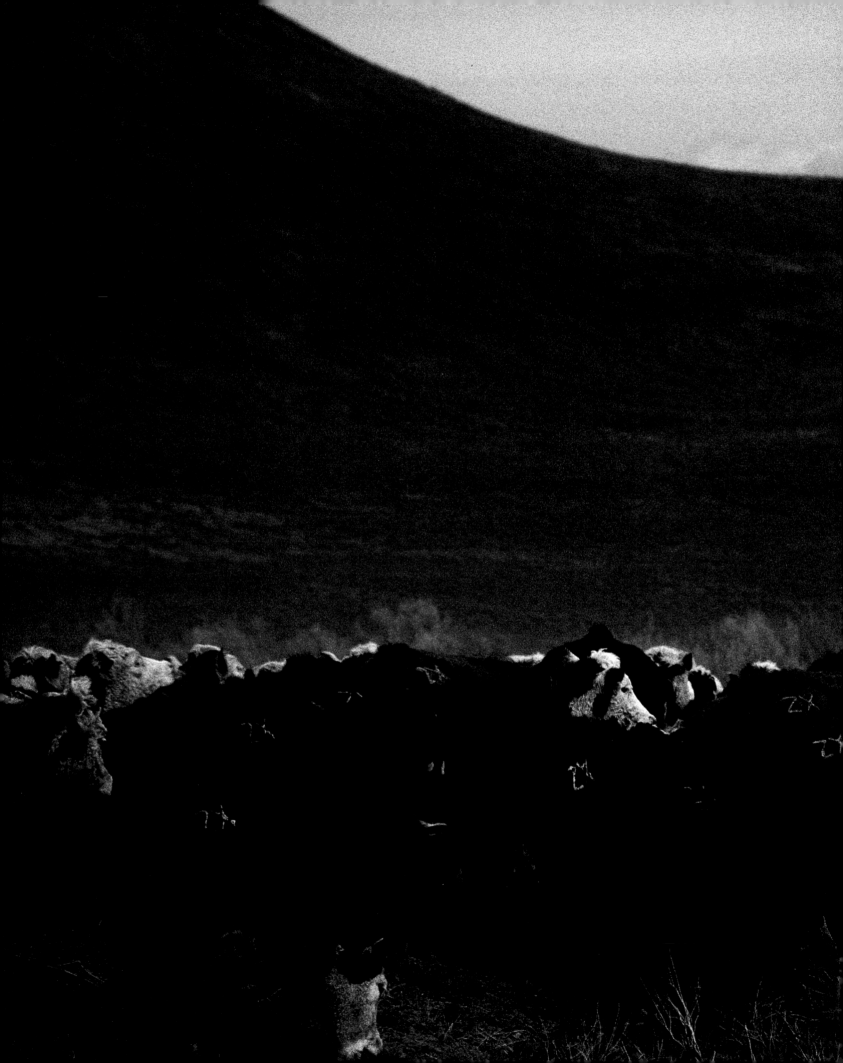

JACK WALTHER

NEVADA

Jack Walther, photograph by Peter de Lory

Jack Walther has been writing and reciting poetry since the 1950s. He has worked on and owned ranches in Elko County, Nevada, and enjoys a national reputation as a workhorse trainer. His poetry deals with events on his ranch near the Ruby Mountains, with stories heard from neighbors, and in some cases with his wife, Irene, whose mastery of ranching, Jack says, is as good as it gets. "Irene and I are life-long ranchers by choice. I enjoy each day doing what I like best. Irene shares the same interests and appreciation of this kind of life. She enjoys her art work and we work together to restore buggies, break horses, and do general ranch work." Jack is a well-known reciter of traditional cowboy poetry, especially the poems of Curley Fletcher and Bruce Kiskaddon. "I write poetry to illustrate a happening, a situation, or a joke," Jack notes in the second edition of his anthology, Ruby Mountain Rhymes. "Free verse and unrhymed poems are not my type."

— CD TRACK 1

THE SHEEP-HERDER'S LAMENT

Written by one of the classic cowboy poets, Curley Fletcher, this poem is a favorite of Jack's to recite.
It never fails to draw out sympathetic shepherds from the crowd.

I have summered in the tropics,
With the yellow fever chill;
I have been down with the scurvy;
I've had every ache and ill.

I have wintered in the Arctic,
Frost-bitten to the bone;
I've been in a Chinese dungeon,
Where I spent a year alone.

I've been shanghaied on a whaler;
And was stranded on the deep,
But I never knew what misery was,
Till I started herding sheep.

The camp boss now is two weeks late,
The burro dead three days.
The dogs are all sore footed, but
The sheep have got to graze.

They won't bed down till after dark,
And they're off before the dawn;
With their baaing and their blatting
They are scattered and they're gone.

I smell their wooly stink all day
And I hear them in my sleep;
Oh, I never knew what misery was,
Till I started herding sheep.

My feet are sore, my boots are worn out;
I'm afraid I'll never mend;
I've got to where a horny-toad
Looks like a long lost friend.

The Spanish Inquisition might
Have been a whole lot worse,
If instead of crucifixion, they
Had had some sheep to nurse.

Old Job had lots of patience, but
He got off pretty cheap –
He never knew what misery was,
For he never herded sheep.

It's nice enough to tell the kids,
Of the big old horny ram,
The gentle soft-eyed mother ewe,
And the wooly little lamb.

It's nice to have your mutton chops,
And your woolen clothes to wear,
But you never stop to give a thought
To the man that put them there.

The blind and deaf are blessed,
The cripples, too, that creep;
They'll never know what misery is,
For they never will herd sheep.

RUBY MOUNTAINS

The majestic peaks of the Ruby Mountains can be seen clearly from Jack's ranch.

I am part of this range of waving grass,
Part of the evening breeze, the gentle rains that pass.
I am the horse or range cow that moves out there so free.
Deep down within, they seem a part of me.

I am the snows on the mountain that cause the streams to flow,
Spreading out on the valley, urging the grass to grow.
The meadow in the valley, the leaves and branches of a tree,
They are more than a thing of beauty. They are a part of me.

I am the buttercups blooming in the springtime,
The call of the blue grouse on the hill,
The peace and quiet of a summer night
When all the world is still.

I am the sparkling stars on a winter night,
Or a crisp cold morning sun.
I am the gurgling protesting stream,
Beneath the winter ice shall run.

The coyote that howls in the evening or the hoot owl in the wood,
I sense them stir within my soul. Deep down it feels so good.
With this all a part of me, I can never be alone.
I am the richest man on earth, for all this I own.

When this body that you see is stilled,
Stand not by my grave and cry.
When a part of all these things,
I will be renewed and shall never die.

But come out in the fresh spring grass,
See the songbirds up in the tree,
Just relax, spend some time.
It is there I shall forever be.

Whitehorse Ranch, Fields, Oregon, photograph by Kurt Markus

BUCK RAMSEY

TEXAS

Buck Ramsey, photograph by Peter de Lory

A Texan from Amarillo, Buck spent his cowboy days snapping out broncs on ranches along the Canadian River in the Texas Panhandle. "For some years back there I rode among the princes of the earth full of health and hell and thinking punching cows was the one big show in the world." When he was thrown from a horse and put in a wheelchair Buck began to write about the cowboy life. A poet, musician, and singer, Buck has used his many talents to enliven traditional and contemporary cowboy culture. An album of traditional cowboy songs, Rolling Uphill from Texas, *came out in 1992 with Fiel Publications, Inc. His epic poem,* And As I Rode Out on the Morning, *was published in 1993 by Texas Tech University Press.* — CD TRACK 2

THE BASS SINGER

A kid from a poor family never feels more highly regarded than when there is a death in the family. That is probably about as close as he will ever come to feeling like royalty. The more tragic the death, the more regal he might feel. My baby sister, at three years old, was just at that age to be the most precious among us, so there could not be a more tragic loss where we were concerned than when she died.

A family deep in mourning, we are lined along the interior wall of the living room where old portraits hang in hardwood oval frames with convex glass covers, faces of dead ancestors somber as our own. My daddy stands behind my mother, seated in a straightbacked dining chair, and we children stand stairstepped with a sudden dropoff where the last step should be, and neighbors, come to call, pass before us with quiet words and gentle gestures so respectful and humble, they could be subjects paying regal homage.

Surely I am as sad as the others. But made proud, too, by this attention. And then so guilty from this elevated notion so out of place. And, too, only yesterday I was the fulcrum of this fetching brood, the brother center embraced and set off by three siblings to the side. The added intrusion of this lost conceit churns with the guilt behind the vulnerable dam that is my young conscience, then a tide bursts loose and washes away the elevating underpinnings and I rush from the room.

Nothing had ever hit me so hard as news of my little sister's death. Strangely, no one was there when my four sisters and I arrived home in the school bus, and the air grew thicker with dread in that lengthening absence of Momma and Daddy and the babies of the family, Winston and Patricia, both too young for school. It was a hot day and I cooled my cheek on the sucker rod pipe of the windmill by the well house as Mrs. Murchison, our nearest neighbor, parked by the side gate to enter the yard. Mr. Murchison remained seated in the car, on the passenger side since he would not drive a motor vehicle, and I caught his eye only long enough to recognize that he had something to say he could not tell me and was in anguish about it. Mary, the youngest of my older sisters, met Mrs. Murchison in the yard and she embraced my sister and told her something which caused Mary to rush into the house, leaving a great wake of emotion, and when Mrs. Murchison looked about and saw me standing alone by the windmill she came to me. I was pressing myself to the pipe so hard it hurt my cheek, but when she called my name and beckoned to me I let loose and went to her, for I loved her very much, and she took me in her arms and told me the sad news. The breath seemed knocked out of me, causing sobbing noises I had never heard from myself. I was embarrassed to so lose control. Then I was ashamed that embarrassment eclipsed my grief. Shame seemed to double my grief. What unfitting thoughts one might recall from his most tragic moments.

I started to go to Mr. Murchison, but he was looking away so I ran for the corral to be with the horses. I called their names and rubbed their sleek coats and great muscles and they hovered about me like older comrades around a young friend needing solace. I straddled the back of my favorite and wept in its mane, and I fell asleep and lay there for some time. I think back and wonder how long the old fellow stood there without making a move that would have disturbed me as I drew comfort from its great old back. I was awakened by the clamor of empty milk buckets and the voice of my mother, strange in its terrible sadness and strange because I had never known her voice there in the corrals where she never came.

It occurred to me Daddy started the chores without me, without even calling out for me to throw in and do my part. If ever, given the chance, I would shirk any duty, it was milking the cows. But again that clean, hard grief crowded me toward virtue and I rushed toward the sound of the buckets to fill my place. My mother's voice, though, coming through the wall of the milkshed stopped me at the boardrail fence of the milkpen, and I stayed away as my daddy did the chores then and each morning and evening until the day after the funeral, because even though my mother had not been to the cowlot with my daddy within memory, she would follow him talking, talking on as he went about his rounds. In sorting out our pasts as all families do, I learned later that Daddy thought it best to coax her into talking her grief away and that they slept only in fitful naps those few days and nights, the lava flow from her erupting heart covering the place over as she followed him about, stooping beside him while he milked the cows, double-stepping to stay apace his long strides as the buckets full of milk swinging at his side locomoted him to the milkroom off the kitchen porch. In one of those recollections years later, I recalled to Daddy almost light-heartedly, that was the only time I got out of milking with never a word said. And my daddy remembered, "But you kept the hayracks full for the first time without being told even once." And so I had, trying to square my conscience.

W hen I rush from the room of caressing looks and murmurs sustaining our noble sadness, I follow the circle of passages around to the bedroom adjoining the living room where I can lie on the cool hardwood floor and watch the scene from under the crack of the door. It is the front bedroom and its north windows look out upon the front yard, almost never entered as ours is a ranch house where all the coming and going is at the back. I do not lie down by the door for I have glanced out a window and think I see, against the last light of the hour after sundown, the roundbellied profile of Mr. Broadfoot, the school teacher, standing statue still by a dwarf elm as if relieving himself on it. But it is not Mr. Broadfoot at all. It is Mr. Murchison standing there still and solitary as if lost in thought. How can two men of such different substance be so alike in outline? Some need to apologize to my beloved old friend sends me scampering back to the living room and my place with my family, for the idea I carry back with me seems so wonderful it might wash all the guilty stains away and leave my mourning pure.

I try to take my place back without notice, then I slip up the line and kneel by my mother's side. Her hands wrestle around in her floursack lap as she unravels her sadness in the monotone I heard through the milkshed wall.

". . . I know He gave us the sunshine to brighten our lives awhile, but He must have surely known how we would wilt with the sunshine gone . . ." she is saying to a neighbor, though not looking at her, or at anything.

The look from the neighbor embraces me tenderly. "But still you have these wonderful children."

"Yes. Our wonderful children. That is what I try to think about. But I can't seem to think of them without thinking of Patricia, and I find that the power of grief is not diluted by the number of those who share it, but multiplied. You grieve at your own loss and for that of those you love. If it were just my own I could hold it in, but it seems to swell in all of us until it bursts out in me and . . . ." She is doing what Daddy told her to do, talking, talking it all out.

I draw close and whisper in her ear. "Momma, ask Mr. Murchison to come to the church and help with the singing." This whispered suggestion is not, for her, in the flow of things, and she looks at me perplexed.

"What is it Sweeney?" Daddy asks.

"Daddy, Mr. Murchison is outside there. Maybe we could get him to come to the church for the funeral and help with the singing."

"He doesn't sing anymore Sweeney. He quit singing a long time ago. You know that."

"But he sings. He still hums the songs. I hear him all the time."

"Not in front of people. Not in public. Maybe to himself or to you."

My mother smiles and something seems lifted from us for a moment. "Yes, Lucas, do you remember? It took the whole church singing the other parts to balance out Claude Murchison's big bass voice." She turns to me. "Go ask Clair Murchison if she will come and let me have a word with her." I go to find Mrs. Murchison as Momma talks on of her husband's big bass voice. ". . . remember how he pushed so with his bass part the rest of us sang louder to even out the other parts until the church's roof and walls seemed threatened with sound . . . ?"

I return with Mrs. Murchison by the hand. "Yes, Clair," Momma says, "just a word with you. We were just now talking about how wonderful it would be if the music for Patricia could be the way it was when Claude was going to church, and what a joy it would be to hear him in the congregation boosting those hymns up like he did when we all went to church and worshiped together."

It is an awkward moment for Mrs. Murchison. Everyone here knows Mr. Murchison avoids community socials and public events, and it is so notoriously the fact that he won't set foot in the church-house anymore, even the children are aware of it,

though none of us are clear about the reason why.

Momma begins focusing in on the things around her.

"Did Claude come with you, Clair? If he is here, I will have Lucas say something to him about it. Lucas would know what to say to him."

"He came with me, but . . . well, you know how Claude is. When he saw all those cars he said, 'Mother, looks like a church parking lot.' When he looked in the window and saw the people milling, he turned back and went to the car. He said he would wait out there a while and come say something to you when the crowd thins out. You know how he is. He means well and thinks so much of your family. Maybe he will come in later and Lucas can say something to him."

"I know where he is. I can go get him, or I can talk to him about it," I say. But it has already become an adult matter and they will have no more of my suggestions.

So I again slip away from the family, the crowded room, and go out the back door and around the house to see if Mr. Murchison is still standing alone in the front yard. His guttural humming is almost the sound of a happy pig in a wallow or, if you catch the tightness in the voice, like the deep sighs of a nightmare. In all the hours I have listened to his humming, I have never heard it sound like this, so void of melody. When I move forward enough to see him, the old fellow is braced with both hands on the top rail of the yard fence facing where the sun has gone down, holding on to the fence as if a force is oppressing him, coming from out of the glimmering West.

"Happened to a cow of mine one time. Man takes a chance on leaving his place alone like that. . . ." He is muttering to himself. "No telling what God is doing to me while I'm gone. A man forsaken needs to stick close and take care of his own. Might be plumb wiped out. Better be getting home."

"Mr. Murchison," I call to him just loud enough to be heard. He is caught off guard, and a startled sort of grunt escapes.

"It's just me, Sweeney McBride."

"Oh yeah, Sweeney my boy. Heh, heh. Just standing here thinking. Yeah. And I think I saw her there for a minute. That tow-headed baby girl belongs to you folks. That where she sleeps up there?" He points to a second-story window above the front porch.

"Yessir, that's the girls' bedroom."

"Yeah, Sweeney. Appeared to me she come climbing backwards out of that window, and the front of her little dress caught there as she reached for the roof with her little legs, then she turned and looked at me and came baby-walking and smiling to me, waving her arms coming stiff-legged down that slanted roof there till she reached the edge and she took flight and commenced floating up and in two seconds just like the sun had sucked her over the horizon. Happened to a cow of mine one time."

The world has not yet begun to unlearn me. I am a young country boy and all things seem possible. More often in his company than anyone except his family, I am accustomed to hearing all manner of things from Mr. Murchison. Despite, or, perhaps, because of this I love him without complication, and though it occurs to me now and then he is spoken of with different looks and tones by people of our community, I know him to be a wiser, more considerate and entertaining man, a safer and stronger presence than anyone I know who is not a cowboy. I have not yet grown out of that blessed ability to remain unperplexed at the way he is talking.

"Patricia. She died today." My throat knots up again.

"Yeah. Your baby sister. Sweeney's little sister. So pretty. Sweet smiling little thing. Mother said we should come over and see about you. I was . . . waiting to go in and say something to your folks. I was. . . ."

"It's all right for you to wait out here. Daddy said it's to be expected that you would wait outside. They know you don't want to come in with so many people. I think Daddy's going to ask you to come sing at the funeral, Mr. Murchison. Momma said maybe you'd come sing like you used to."

He falls silent except for guttural noises emanating from some interior dialogue with himself or with mysterious forces with whom he sometimes falls into confab. This communion, however, seems to be unusually troublesome and he becomes agitated in a way strange to me.

"No telling what might be happening to me," he says, beginning to stir around nervously. "I need to be getting back home. Need to check on things. Those who would be Godforsaken need to tend their own. Yeah. Say, Sweeney" — he seemed, for my benefit, to gather calm back to himself — "You go tell Mother old Claude said he needs to get himself home. You tell your mother and daddy he said, well, he said he felt great sorrow and would speak to them. Run on. Tell Mother I'll be in the car."

When I go back to the living room I am greeted by kinfolks who have come their distance to be with us. Mrs. Murchison is still talking to Momma, and it turns out arrangements have been made for me to go home with the Murchisons to make some room for company. One of my sisters goes upstairs with me to get some clothes (sad, sad looks, light touches, silently we linger in communion closer than we will ever know again), and soon the three of us are on our way out of the breaks those few miles to the Murchison place where the flat plain begins. Mr. Murchison has not touched the steering wheel of a car since some "time of his troubles" still vague to me, but he urges his wife to drive much faster on those dirt roads than she wants to and he leans forward, straining his vision to see beyond the headlight beams, and he makes signs and sounds of relief when the outline of their farm appears.

Channing, Texas, watercolor by William Matthews

We park by the yard gate leading to the back door of their house. "Mother, I've got to look around, check things out," Mr. Murchison says. "You go in. I won't be long."

She gives him one of those wonderful looks country women give their husbands when they are burdened, a look at the same time stoic and deeply concerned. "Come to the kitchen and get a lantern," she says. "Sweeney can go with you to hold the light." She is concerned he might get involved with some of those spiritual agents God sometimes sends to deal with him and that he might stay gone for hours guarding against their forays and assaults.

We go to the barn and I hold the lantern as he makes his inspection. He could, if necessary, feel his way around in the dark, because he built the place with the help of his older sons. He checks to see if the main joints are still flush and tight, the joists plumb and stout, checks the gear in the tackroom to see if leather lines or couplings have dried and

cracked with a day's inattention. His milk cows are penned and their bags are filling, the calves safe and separate in their pens, so the corral fences are still standing with the gates closed. His pigs grunt soft in dreams, there is peace in the henhouse, the machinery is lined neat as a military formation, and the windmill struggles slowly up and coasts down in its pumping cycle, its tin places clanging quietly with a slight shift of the breeze.

"It's a nice night, Mother, you should already be in bed asleep," he says as we enter the kitchen. But she has waited up to talk with him, and they bed me in the room off the kitchen where Nate and I often sleep together.

Though two years older than me and a farmer's boy, their son, Nate, is my best friend. Even at this early age, I am conditioned to a deep and abiding prejudice for grass and see heresy in what would destroy it or keep it from growing, so already I carry some disdain for the nester plowman. This does not extend to the Murchison family, however, and I, with just a little bit of guilt for betraying the cowboy calling, feel something between respect and awe for Nate's easy grace with machinery, his gift for building and repair.

These skills account for his absence. He is downstate representing our school's 4-H Club in some kind of contest involving tractor skills. I feel relieved that he does not have to be here to deal with my sadness, or that I am not required to set him at ease with my grief. I am glad to have this quiet place to myself. But still I hear them talking low in the kitchen.

"Poppa, Lucas and Dory said to mention to you how nice it would be if you could go to the funeral and maybe help with the singing. You know I don't have to make explanations or excuses to them. They understand this thing with you. They will not feel badly toward you in the least if you don't see your way clear to go."

"Yes, Mother, I saw that precious baby, their darling little girl, her stiff little waddle, the waving and reaching of her arms as she came for me and disappeared. And the boy, he came out there and mentioned something about that to me. His voice was so sad and quiet it bent and broke. It tugged at my heart, Mother, I tell you. Maybe. I don't know."

I cry myself to sleep and wake sometime in the night to the gentle sound of rain. It is a good grass rain, a slow-soaker, and the timing is good for the wheat crop.

As we age we ponder and piece together the history of our place and of those close to us. This is the way I have sorted out the history and circumstances of our little community in those days to come to an understanding of how Mr. Murchison came to be the manner of man he was when I knew him.

Back in the days when Claude Murchison was a deacon in the Clearwell Community Primitive Baptist Church he had been a mediocre farmer, for his best labor went into his work for the Lord. Although now he was considered at best the community eccentric and at worst plumb loony, he was also grudgingly given up to be the best farmer around, for his anxious labor with crops and livestock was inspired by a kind of motto hanging on the wall of his mind to the effect if a man is on his own he's got to do things right.

He did not know, nor did anyone, what happened back in that time to begin the decline in church attendance. But if the cause was God's own mystery, the effect was apparent to everyone. Deacon Murchison, for his part, was determined to fill the space and silence of the dwindling congregation with the joyful noise of his own worship, and as his manner of worship was mainly in song, he sought to enliven the languoring flock by raising the volume of his voice, eager that the Lord should have to listen no harder than ever to get the message from Clearwell Church. In unkind truth, this ardor of his began to embarrass the other church members and made their worship more timid, so it can be said his zeal further wore away at the eroding chunk of the community worshipping God on Sundays. As the benches grew emptier of a Sunday morning and the greater space echoed louder with Deacon Murchison's musical praise, a new pastor was called.

The new preacher right away thought he saw the cause of the problem. "Unfortunately," he said, as so many had said before him, "in matters concerning the work of the Lord we must often judge harshly." Confiding one Sunday in young Brother Broadfoot, the school teacher with whom he felt kindred in community leadership, he said, "That Brother Murchison is a raving lunatic, an embarrassment to the Lord and His church, though I suppose Christian charity forces me to admit that he might mean well.

For the first time I wish we Primitive Baptists believed in passing the plate so we could call on him to count the money during singing. I have in mind to see if I can find some janitor work to keep him busy so the rest of us can worship the Lord in peace and dignity."

The teacher's belly shook with laughter as he added, "If you'll forgive a slightly off-color observation, Preacher, all of us around here — considering the way he acts and sings — we often say old Claude Murchison must have the brains of a bat and the balls of a bull."

These remarks were made as the two men approached the three-holer toilet behind the church, and when they opened its door they saw Deacon Murchison sitting red of face on the middle hole. They declined the outer holes. And when Claude Murchison was finished with his toilet, he was finished with his church, the place of his love and labor and rejoicing, the mooring of his soul and sanity.

In time he had mustered the courage to curse the Lord in timid ways, and he grew to think of himself as a poor nester harried by the Lord, who in his mind had taken on the character of a giant rancher surrounding his place and threatening his ruin. Forsaken by his father, he felt himself an orphan among men. He clove only to his place and his family until I began my visits to their home.

While the Murchison farm was on flat, tillable land, our ranch spread in the breaks of a river slope where the land was untillable and blessedly left to grass. My daddy didn't want pigs and chickens on the place as long as we could get bacon and eggs elsewhere, so we bought these staples from the Murchisons. From the time I was old enough to go out horseback alone, I was occasionally sent riding for the bacon and eggs. When I started to school, their youngest son became my mentor and best friend. They had other children grown and gone from home, so although Nate was one of those unplanned children come lately, he turned out to be a special blessing without whom Mr. Murchison, in the addled state he had come to, could not have kept the farm up, for he could or would not drive away from their place or deal with other people.

In those days out in the country, the highest form of social activity with a friend was spending the night as a guest in his home. If ever I spent a night away from home, it was with Nate. It would have been unthinkable not to throw in and help with chores, so over the years I became as familiar with the routine of daily chores on their place as I was on our own. Also in those days in the country, much of the relationship father to son was as bossman to worker, so it was not unusual for one of those rural fathers to be more open and playful with a neighbor's son than with his own. I can see now that it raised Mr. Murchison's spirits for me to be around, and, far from being resentful, Nate, as well as his mother, appreciated my friendship with Mr. Murchison and enjoyed his enlivened spirit when I was in their company.

He seemed to hum endlessly, and I grew to realize he was humming the bass lines to the old hymns he sang with such enthusiasm in his church days. But the few times I started singing a melody with him, he stopped his humming and looked at me strangely and asked me why I didn't sing some of the happy songs that came over the radio "instead of old churchy stuff." Then after a moment of silence, he would begin humming the hymns again.

I liked listening to him, and liked it best when he hummed away at milking time, for he milked inside his barn and from that cavern his big bass voice came sounding like the long pipes of an organ in a tabernacle. I knew very well how the old hymns were supposed to sound because my sisters sang like angels and harmonized their four parts around our home and often for public occasions, especially at church, and as I listened to the old man's voice come boom-

Hogback Orchard, watercolor by William Matthews

ing out of the barn I would try in my mind to build many voices of the other three parts on top of his bass line and wonder what music put together like that must sound like.

I was in my teens before it dawned on me that there was something out of the ordinary about Mr. Murchison besides this perpetual music of his, those meandering monologues, the great friendliness he showed me, and some core of wisdom he seemed to be offering me. Exposure to community gossip and that inevitable narrowing of mature observation, of course, finally made me aware that he was quite different, and could not be regarded as someone with whom one should be expected to carry on normally. But still I enjoyed being with him, and in fact grew closer to him when Nate graduated from high school

and went away to college, for in the two years before I went away I would go over and help him by doing some of the work Nate had done. As I grew more and more into the cowboy way, I avoided farming. But he still fed with the last team of horses used in that part of the country, and I enjoyed being with that fine old pair and riding on the feed wagon with my old friend. I'm sure it was during those times I pieced together much of his past, and from those long visits I gained an impression of the turn of events in their home that day of my little sister's funeral.

He talked of that fine rain with his wife. He went out to count his cattle, and the count turned out right because a neighbor had put back a stray he thought had wandered off over the horizon.

Everything seemed so right and in order, there was some suggestion in his conversation with Mrs. Murchison that God was calling some kind of truce, perhaps offering something of an apology, and all of this came to be connected in his mind with the death of my little sister and that strange suggestion about going to her funeral and joining in the singing of the old songs.

So he went digging around for his high-top black shoes and a tie and coat he might put with his khaki shirt and britches to look dressed up enough for church. "Mother," he said as she made these things ready to wear and helped to fit them to him as best she could, "there's no need for crying now. Nothing to make a fuss over. We'll just go play our little part the way they would want us to."

As holiday dances are not allowed here, the church is full as only a funeral can make it. I sit in my place with my family, surely the only one here who holds out any expectation — perhaps the only one who has ever entertained any expectation — that Mr. Murchison will come. The singing starts with "Amazing Grace," and as I am about ready to let my disappointment fade into my other sorrow there is a noticeable faltering of the assembled voices on "... was blind but now I see ..." and the embarrassed emptiness of a few missed beats by the song leader before the next verse begins.

I turn and see Mr. Murchison and his wife entering the church, and it does not even occur to me to feel guilty about this moment of joy. A man in back of the congregation offers him a song book. He declines it, stands looking as if he is alone in this crowd, then softens, merges, and begins humming the bass lines. Soon he is singing the words, and as his voice grows stronger the other singers raise the sound of their voices and the people who haven't been singing, who haven't sung for years, take song books from the benchback racks or look on the books of neighbors to join in. By the time six verses of "Amazing Grace" are sung, everyone there knows something old and unusual is happening.

I am looking to the back of the church with a big smile of happiness on my face. My sister tugs at my sleeve, calling my attention to Daddy motioning to me, but by now my joy and sorrow have stirred to a pure potion immune to any guilt and, sure enough, all stays well with my soul, for it turns out my daddy beckons to me because Momma has made a list of songs and wants me to take it to the song leader standing in front of the little mound of flowers. During "Angel Band," my sisters, with my parents' blessings, join the singing, and a shifting around of parts, a levelling of harmony begins, and the men who have been singing bass find the foundation there strong enough without them and wander through the passages till they find the places where they can help best with the framing and filling and texturing out, and the parts grow in strength through "Where the Soul Never Dies," "Jesus, Lover of My Soul," "How Firm a Foundation," and other selections till, finally, in an ancient and intricate Sacred Harp number, the memory of their old music comes back complete. And when the old bass singer, ringing alone on his part, begins solo on the refrain:

"Jesus can make a dying bed
Feel soft as downy pillows are
While on His breast I lean my head
And breathe my life out sweetly there."

the tenors and altos and singers of the melody aspire up around him in sturdy counterpoint, reaching my little sister's temple to the sky.

A look of peace comes over my mother's face as she leans her head on my daddy's shoulder, and he, for the first time, begins softly to cry. The sermon is brief. ◆

ANTHEM

These seven stanzas serve as an introduction to Buck's sixty-page poem,
And As I Rode Out on the Morning, *which tells of the apprenticeship of a young cowboy.*

And in the morning I was riding
Out through the breaks of that long plain,
And leather creaking in the quieting
Would sound with trot and trot again.
I lived in time with horse hoof falling;
I listened well and heard the calling
The earth, my mother, bade to me,
Though I would still ride wild and free.
And as I flew out on the morning,
Before the bird, before the dawn,
I was the poem, I was the song.
My heart would beat the world a warning —
Those horsemen now rode all with me,
And we were good, and we were free.

We were not told, but ours the knowing
We were the native strangers there
Among the things the land was growing —
To know this gave us more the care
To let the grass keep at its growing
And let the streams keep at their flowing.
We knew the land would not be ours,
That no one has the awful pow'rs
To claim the vast and common nesting,
To own the life that gave him birth,
Much less to rape his mother earth
And ask her for a mother's blessing
And ever live in peace with her,
And, dying, come to rest with her.

Oh, we would ride and we would listen
And hear the message on the wind.
The grass in morning dew would glisten
Until the sun would dry and blend
The grass to ground and air to skying.
We'd know by bird or insect flying
Or by their mood or by their song
If time and moon were right or wrong
For fitting works and rounds to weather.
The critter coats and leaves of trees
Might flash some signal with a breeze —
Or wind and sun on flow'r or feather.
We knew our way from dawn to dawn,
And far beyond, and far beyond.

It was the old ones with me riding
Out through the fog fall of dawn,
And they would press me to deciding
If we were right or we were wrong.
For time came we were punching cattle
For men who knew not spur nor saddle,
Who came with locusts in their purse
To scatter loose upon the earth.
The savage had not found this prairie
Till some who hired us came this way
To make the grasses pay and pay
For some raw greed no wise or wary
Regard for grass could satisfy.
The old ones wept, and so did I.

Do you remember? We'd come jogging
To town with jingle in our jeans,
And in the wild night we'd be bogging
Up to our hats in last month's dreams.
It seemed the night could barely hold us
With all those spirits to embold' us
While, horses waiting on three legs,
We'd drain the night down to the dregs.
And just before beyond redemption
We'd gather back to what we were.
We'd leave the money left us there
And head our horses for the wagon.
But in the ruckus, in the whirl,
We were the wolves of all the world.

The grass was growing scarce for grazing,
Would soon turn sod or soon turn bare.
The money men set to replacing
The good and true in spirit there.
We could not say, there was no knowing,
How ill the future winds were blowing.
Some cowboys even shunned the ways

Of cowboys in the trail herd days
(But where's the gift not turned for plunder?),
Forgot that we are what we do
And not the stuff we lay claim to.
I dream the spell that we were under;
I throw in with a cowboy band
And go out horseback through the land.

So mornings now I'll go out riding
Through pastures of my solemn plain,
And leather creaking in the quieting
Will sound with trot and trot again.
I'll live in time with horse hoof falling;
I'll listen well and hear the calling
The earth, my mother, bids to me,
Though I will still ride wild and free.
And as I ride out on the morning
Before the bird, before the dawn,
I'll be this poem, I'll be this song.
My heart will beat the world a warning —
Those horsemen will ride all with me,
And we'll be good, and we'll be free.

Repose, watercolor by William Matthews

SUNNY HANCOCK

OREGON

Sunny Hancock, photograph by Peter de Lory

Sunny lives in Lakeview, Oregon, with his wife, Alice. Born and raised on a ranch near Williams, Arizona, he cowboyed in several states before settling in southern Oregon. "I finished my buckaroo career up as a cow boss for the ZX outfit in Paisley, Oregon," Sunny notes. "Then my wife and I bought a little place of our own. It really couldn't be construed as a ranch as we never had over a hundred and fifty head of cattle. That's when my logging career started as I had to go to work in the woods to support those old cows." Sunny is known for his strong level gaze and iron-trap mind for remembering recitations. He knows poems from both the cowboy and logging traditions. In recent years he has been writing narrative poems as well as political verse, expressing his beliefs about issues ranging from spotted owls to ranchers' rights. He has made a cassette of recitations entitled Cowboy Poetry, New and Used, *published by Outhouse Enterprises, Lakeview, Oregon.* — CD TRACK 3

WHEN THEY'VE FINISHED SHIPPING CATTLE IN THE FALL

*Written in the 1920s by Bruce Kiskaddon, this classic poem is often recited by Sunny
who first heard it while following an old wagon back to the ranch at the age of seventeen.*

Though you're not exactly blue,
Yet you don't feel like you do
In the winter, or the long hot summer days.
For your feelin's and the weather
Seem to sort of go together,
And you're quiet in the dreamy autumn haze.
When the last big steer is goaded
Down the chute, and safely loaded;
And the summer crew has ceased to hit the ball;
When a feller starts a draggin'
To the home ranch with the wagon —
When they've finished shippin' cattle in the fall.

Only two men left a standin'
On the job for winter brandin',
And your pardner he's a loafin' at your side.
With a bran new saddle creakin',
Neither one of you is speakin',
And you feel it's goin' to be a silent ride.
But you savvy one another,
For you know him like a brother.
He is friendly but he's quiet, that is all;
He is thinkin' while he's draggin'
To the home ranch with the wagon —
When they've finished shippin' cattle in the fall.

And the saddle hosses stringin'
At an easy walk a swingin'
In behind the old chuck wagon movin' slow.
They are weary gaunt and jaded
With the mud and brush they've waded,
And they settled down to business long ago.
Not a hoss is feelin' sporty,

Not a hoss is actin' snorty;
In the spring the brutes was full of buck and bawl;
But they're gentle, when they're draggin'
To the home ranch with the wagon —
When they've finished shippin' cattle in the fall.

And the cook leads the retreat
Up there on his wagon seat,
With his hat pulled way down forrud on his head.
Used to make that old team hustle,
Now he hardly moves a muscle,
And a feller might imagine he was dead,
'Cept his old cob pope is smokin'
As he lets his team go pokin'
Hittin' all the humps and hollers in the road.
No the cook has not been drinkin'
He's just settin' there and thinkin'
'Bout the places and the people that he knowed
You can see the dust a trailin'
And two little clouds a sailin',
And a big mirage like lakes and timber tall.
It's sorta' lonesome when you're dreggin'
To the home ranch with the wagon —
When they've finished shippin' cattle in the fall.

When you make the camp that night,
Though the fire is burnin' bright,
Yet nobody seems to have a lot to say.
In the spring you sung and hollered,
Now you git your supper swallered
And you crawl into your blankets right away.

Then you watch the stars a shinin'
Up there in the soft blue linin'
And you sniff the frosty night air clear and cool.
You can hear the night hoss shiftin'
And your memory starts a driftin'
To the little village where you went to school.

With its narrow gravel streets
And the kids you used to meet,
And the common where you used to play baseball.
Now you're far away and draggin'
To the home ranch with the wagon —
For they've finished shippin' cattle in the fall.

And your school boy sweetheart too,
With her eyes of honest blue —
Best performer in the old home talent show.
You was nothin' but a kid
But you liked her, sure you did —
Lord! And that was over thirty years ago.
Then your memory starts to roam
From Old Mexico to Nome.
From the Rio Grande to the Powder River,
Of the things you seen and done,
Some of them was lots of fun
And a lot of other things they make you shiver.
'Bout that boy by name of Reid
That was killed in a stampede,
'Twas away up north you helped to dig his grave,
And your old friend Jim the boss
That got tangled with a hoss,
And the fellers couldn't reach in time to save.

You was there when Ed got hisn,
Boy that killed him's still in prison,
And old Lucky George is rich and livin' high.
Poor old Tom, he come off worst,
Got his leg broke, died of thirst,
Lord but that must be an awful way to die.

Then them winters at the ranches,
And the old time country dances,
Everybody there was sociable and gay.
Used to lead 'em down the middle
Jest a prancin' to the fiddle,
Never thought of going home till the break of day.

No there ain't no chance for sleepin'
For the memories come a creepin'
And sometimes you think you hear the voices call;
When a feller starts a draggin'
To the home ranch with the wagon —
When they've finished shippin' cattle in the fall.

Ricky Morris and Sam Redding, Susan Valley Ranch, California, photograph by Jay Dusard

Resting, photograph by Bank Langmore

ALONE

*"Nobody gets into the mind of a cowboy like Bruce Kiskaddon," Sunny notes.
This is another of Sunny's recital favorites by the classic cowboy poet who died in 1950.*

The hills git awful quiet, when you have to camp alone.
It's mighty apt to set a feller thinkin'.
You always half way waken when a hoss shoe hits a stone,
Or you hear the sound of hobble chains a clinkin'.

It is then you know the idees that you really have in mind.
You think about the things you've done and said.
And you sometimes change the records that you nearly always find
In the back of almost every cow boy's head.

It gives a man a soter different feelin' in his heart.
And he sometimes gits a little touch of shame,
When he minds the times and places that he didn't act so smart,
And he knows himself he played a sorry game.

It kinda makes you see yourself through other people's eyes.
And mebby so yore pride gits quite a fall.
When yore all alone and thinkin', well, you come to realize
Yo're a mighty common feller after all.

OVERLEAF: IL Ranch, Tuscarora, Nevada, photograph by Kurt Markus

SUNNY HANCOCK

TERESA JORDAN

WYOMING

Teresa Jordan, photograph by Peter de Lory

Teresa was raised as part of the fourth generation on a ranch in the Iron Mountain country of southeastern Wyoming. The ranch was sold in 1978, and Teresa has studied and written about rural culture ever since. Her first book, Cowgirls, Women of the American West, *now reprinted by University of Nebraska Press, grew out of hundreds of hours of interviews with women on ranches and in the rodeo. Her most recent book,* Riding the White Horse Home, *published by Pantheon in 1993, is a memoir in which the stories of her family and the Iron Mountain community serve as a lens through which to see the larger issues of the West. Her fiction, essays, and poetry have appeared in national magazines and newspapers. Teresa now lives in Starr Valley, Nevada.* — CD TRACK 4

KELLEY

From Teresa's book of memoirs, Riding the White Horse Home

When I was little, an old man by the name of Kelley worked for us. He was not a cowboy, which is to say he didn't ride. Rather, he was the chore boy, which meant he did everything else. He tended the garden, cut the lawn, milked the cow, fed the chickens, sharpened sickles for the mowing machine, carpentered, plumbed, and fixed fence. Above all, he irrigated. He had an eye for incline and gravity, and in a country where water was precious, he made it go a long way. I once heard it said that Kelley could run water up a witch's tit. Even my grandfather, seldom bent to a compliment, said Kelley was the only one who really understood water on the Jordan Ranch.

Kelley was my friend. He took me with him everywhere and I loved him. He never talked much, but he chuckled when I said something clever and he let me shift the Jeep while he clutched.

I have a hard time visualizing him now. Small details come into focus — his heavy lace-up work boots, the frayed cuffs of his Levi's, his flannel shirts, the flash of red from his pouch of Beech-Nut chewing tobacco — but I can't remember his face. It's almost as if I were too small to step back and take him in whole. Mostly, I remember his hands, the pure white hair on the backs of his broad stubby fingers, the cracked thumbnails imbedded with fine dark lines, the deep scab on the break of one knuckle, the blue veins that rose so distinctly as he gripped a shovel handle or a steering wheel.

His hands were always in motion and there was something rhythmic about them. I loved to watch him sharpen sickles. The sharpening wheel sat in the darkest part of the barn, and each time Kelley brought one of the triangular blades to the wheel, sparks flew in an arc. I could watch that curve of orange stars for hours, and the sweet, sweeeet, sweeeet whine of metal against stone would draw me from wherever I might be playing to take up my seat on a milking stool in the cool shadows. I was a talkative kid, but I kept my silence when Kelley sharpened sickles. The action, so musical and meditative, had the power to cast even me in its spell.

Kelley introduced me to the elemental world. He was the one my brother Blade and I would tell when we found a bull snake. Bull snakes, with their appetite for mice, were precious. "Kelley!" we would yell. "We found you a snake!" The old man would come and peer at it for a moment and then lean down as if to regard it closer. Suddenly, with a motion as quick as a cat's, he would grab it behind the head. Then he would be all slowness and calm again and the bull snake would wrap itself around his arm as if even it knew there was no reason to be afraid. Blade and I would follow Kelley down to the cake shack, the old boxcar on blocks where we stored concentrated feed for the cattle. The dark shack smelled of dust and grain and molasses; sacks of cottonseed cake were stacked up to the ceiling and mouse droppings were scattered everywhere. We would release the bull snake and say, "Good hunting, old fellow. Have a good time."

The first time I caught a bull snake by myself, I ran to Kelley shouting, "Look what I did, Kelley, look what I did!" The snake was big, five or six feet long. It wrapped itself tightly around my arm. I can still feel its muscular grip and the warmth it had picked up from the sun. Kelley nodded appreciatively. "This time," he said, "I'll walk *you* to the cake shack."

Everything Kelley did fascinated me. He fashioned a latch for the chicken coop from a piece of willow and a leather thong. He notched corral poles with a hatchet. He spaded manure into watertight dams, threaded earthworms on hooks, gutted trout, ran his traps.

One night I helped him skin three beavers. Kelley pulled them up from the water and laid them out on the ground. The largest was nearly as big as I was — I must have been five at the time. All three were dark and shiny and had a sense of great mass, something both sad and majestic. I remember wanting to lie down next to them, to cuddle up, to sleep. Kelley squatted next to the largest one for a long time, stroking its dead forehead as he might a dog's.

We skinned out the two smaller ones. My job was to pull back on the pelt as Kelley cut it away from the carcass, and I'd watch the deft flash of his knife as he worked in the moonlight. When he cut into the big beaver, he punctured the bile. The smell was immediate and overpowering — green, black, utterly wretched. I tried to concentrate on other things — the sound of frogs along the creek, the prospect of a trip to town the next day with my mother — but all I wanted to do was cry. Instead, I leaned back as far as I could and tried not to breathe at all. Kelley skinned at arms' length and finally we finished. He threw the pelts into the back of the Jeep and left the carcasses for the coyotes. We got in and he nodded for me to work the gearshift. I shifted into second. When the Jeep jerked forward, he said,

"You're a trooper." He reached into his pocket and brought out a smooth stone. "Here. I found this today." When I got it home under the light, I saw it was sky blue, the color of a robin's egg.

Kelley had a weakness for liquor. He never drank on the ranch. He could have; there was no rule against it. What a man did on his own time was of no concern as long as he turned up sober for work. But Kelley knew that if he took one drink, he was lost. He could stay dry for months at a time, ordering the small extras he wanted from my mother when she went to town: Beech-Nut tobacco, Black Jack gum. But sooner or later he'd get an itch. He'd draw his wages and we wouldn't see him for three or four days, sometimes five. When he'd return, his stubble of beard would have a yellow tint and he'd smell different, sour and old. I'd run up to him like I always did and he'd ruffle my hair, but he wouldn't look me in the eye. He'd talk to my father then, holding his hat in front of him with both hands, fidgeting with its brim. Few words passed between them. They had a perfect understanding. Kelley was welcome here until he started drinking, and then he wasn't.

Usually, when Kelley left us, he'd go to work for the Diamond, a ranch twenty miles further down Chugwater Creek. There he'd stay until his semiannual thirst bounced him back to us. Kelley was a good hand. If my father had a spot for him, he always hired him back.

Until the day he didn't. The last time Kelley came to the door for a job, his eyes were sallow, red in the corners, and there was a sunken look about him. Even the hair on the back of his hands had a yellowish tinge. It was almost noon, but my father hadn't come in yet. My mother sat Kelley down at the kitchen table and gave him a cup of coffee. I bounced down beside him. He gave me a weak grin as he cradled his coffee cup in both hands to keep it from shaking. "How you doin', kid," he said.

My father came in for lunch and he and Kelley went to the desk in the corner of the dining room. I sat on the stairs, half-hidden by the rail, to watch the transaction, the small advance, that would mean my friend was back in my life. There was much low talking and shaking of heads. Nothing changed hands. My father walked Kelley to the door. I stood at the kitchen window and watched him drive off in his little topless Jeep, a single satchel and a few traps in the back, his shoulders hunched to the wheel. ◆

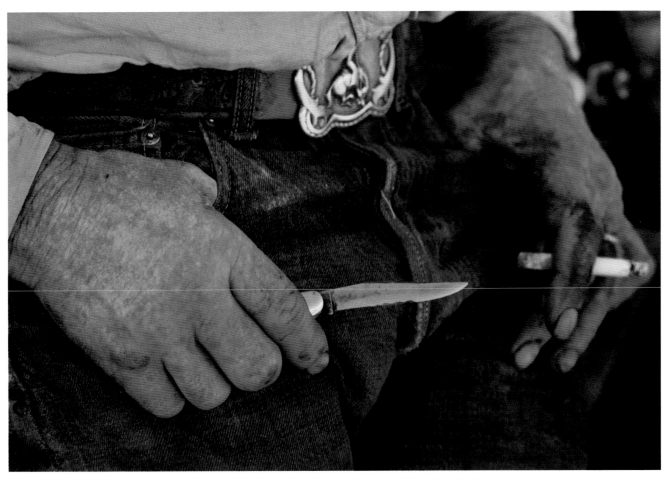

Castration Knife, Branding Time, Montana, photograph by William Albert Allard

Julie Hagen, Wagstaff Land & Cattle Co., Wyoming, photograph by Jay Dusard

OLD ANNE

The arm that hadn't healed right would not bend
to hold a hairbrush.   "Hack it off!"
Old Anne said of her braid, that braid like blood
flung from the heart, so long a part of her,
that thick grey snake slung heavy down her back.
Young Charlotte, wide-eyed Charlotte, stroked the shears,
reached out her hand to touch the braid, drew back —
"Please, child," Anne said, "don't be afraid to help me."
So Charlotte cut, and Old Anne closed her grey
sun-tired eyes. The hacking made her think

of falling, the colt falling, rain-soaked limestone soil
slick as oil — slicker — and a boulder field
cut jagged at the bottom of the hill.
The heavy braid hung loosely now by just a few thin strands;
The scissors sawed one last time through, it fell.
The soft thud she remembered just before
she woke, before the pain set in; the young horse,
stunned, on top of her, had just begun to twitch.

"MY O DERE CHILDREN.
I WISH YOU WERE HEARE."

*Teresa based this poem on letters from Abigail Malick to her family in the States after arriving in
Oregon Territory, 1850 (see note to CD track 4 on page 122).*

I never shal see eney of you eney More
And you never Will see Hiram eney more
He went Aswiming in the Plat
Aswiming and he drounded in the Plat
he swum Acrost the river
Acrost the Fast broad river
he swum until he couldnt Swim
eney more
And the young Men said O hiram Do swim
and Hiram said o my god I cannot
eney More.
One boy took A branch and started to Swim
to him the Water ran too fast.
The young Men said O hiram O Swim
and Hiram said so Loud

it reached the bank
O lord jesus receive My Soul
for I am not
eney More.
So now you know
you need not ask about Him
eney More.
It will not do you
eney Good
to trouble us
about him
eney more.

BEFORE THE PHONE

I was nine years old before I knew a number by heart. I was nine before I needed to. We had no street address, no post office box, no zip code. We were just the Jordans at Iron Mountain and, like the Farthings or the Hirsigs or the Bells, we were easy enough to find.

Before the phone, we drove seven miles to the Post Office for news and got as much as we needed. In emergencies, we drove to Chugwater, twenty-six dirt-road miles away, to use the phone. And if someone had to reach us — really, really had to reach us — they could call the section foreman on the railroad and he'd relay the message.

That's how we learned that my mother's folks had been critically injured in a car crash — a knock on the door in the middle of the night. I remember the way the engineer held his cap in his hand. I remember the soft timbre of his voice. I remember the sound of the train idling on the tracks a half mile away, its long yellow beam cutting into that long lonely night.

This was my first experience with tragedy, with the way a bit of news can change the course of your life, and at least the messenger was kind. It all seemed more reverential, somehow, than news of later losses that jangled us awake so much more abruptly, as if bad news had no face and needed no rail to ride in on.

Hutterite Girl, Montana, photograph by William Albert Allard

OVERLEAF: OO Ranch, Seligman, Arizona, photograph by Kurt Markus

VESS QUINLAN

COLORADO

Vess Quinlan, photograph by Peter de Lory

The great-grandson of a Colorado settler of Irish descent, Vess says he fits right in the state's poorest county, where he lives near Alamosa in an old colonial Spanish farm and ranching community. His family outfit, located at eight thousand feet above sea level, produces alfalfa and winters cattle and sheep on alfalfa clean-up. Vess had been writing — and hiding — his poems since 1960, but went public, along with a lot of other writers, at the first Cowboy Poetry Gathering in Elko, Nevada in 1985. Moving between college, where he studied creative writing, and long-haul trucking, where he augments his income, Vess has written poetry that often deals with the transitions contemporary cowboys are making by moving from country to town. His recent book of poetry, The Trouble with Dreams *(1990), contains accounts of modern ranching life, interspersed with humorous verse. Recently, Vess has been writing prose, penning a series of short stories about Leo, a Spanish-speaking hand who worked with the Quinlans over many years.* — CD TRACK 5

A TRULY DURABLE JOKE

When our hired man, Leo, had worked for us a week or so, he brought a relative to visit.

"Boss, I want you to meet my uncle Placido. He works for the Government," Leo said proudly.

Placido offered a dry knobby hand. I shook it and invited them both in for coffee. Placido was the smallest of Leo's many uncles and the most wrinkled. He fell somewhere in the middle of the age range, having slipped past and headed cheerfully into his eighth decade. A great good humor emanated from his bright brown eyes. He resembled an amused brown elf bent slightly forward by years of hard manual labor.

After a few moments of coffee and polite conversation, the old man got to the point. He made his pitch, so to speak, with the distinctive accent, wonderful word choice, and delightful phrasing of those who, while comfortable with English, really prefer to speak Spanish.

He drew an official-looking document from his pocket and said, "Mr. Quinlan, I have been noticing the prairie dogs are getting pretty bad in that little pasture across the road from your alfalfa. If you will sign this paper, I will cure your land of prairie dogs."

The paper was a two parter from the state agency for predator and pest control. One part required a legal description and granted permission to enter the property. The other part had a blank for the number of acres infested and authorized payment from a special tax paid by livestock growers and farmers. The blank for the legal description and the blank for the number of acres infested had been filled in correctly.

I suspected Mr. Gardunio had cured the little pasture of prairie dogs many times.

"You must sign both places," the old man said, "or the state will not pay me."

I signed both places and said, "I will be pleased to have you cure my land of prairie dogs but if I were you I would not cure the land too hard. I would always leave a few so there will be money for next year."

The old fellow appeared to consider my advice carefully then smiled and said, "That's a pretty good joke for a gringo. And it's true, too."

I guess it was a pretty good joke because it became a ritual and every year, along in May, for over twenty years the little man would knock on my door and we would solemnly repeat it almost word for word until Placido Gardunio, true to his name, died quietly in his sleep one cold January night.

If prairie dogs knew about holidays, they would have declared a big one at the passing of Placido Gardunio (1880-1973) because never again, along in May, would the bent shadow of their number one enemy move slowly from mound to mound with his plastic scoop and little sack of poison pellets.

The prairie dog town prospers in the post-Placido period because the state never replaced him, or any of the other private contractors, choosing instead to expand the bureaucracy and threaten pests and predators with state employees located mostly in downtown Denver.

Fortunately for my alfalfa, owls patrolling the wide county road at night and a trio of golden eagles perched atop the power poles by day have forced expansion of the town westward, away from the alfalfa.

Only brave or foolhardy prairie dogs will risk scampering past the owls at night to gorge on my alfalfa and when they waddle back at daylight, furry bellies stuffed with the forbidden legumes, they make easy picking for the eagles.

I will eventually have to do something about the prolific little devils because they are eating up land like crazed real estate developers.

Should I travel to Denver and wander the halls of state government, I would eventually find a glass door with the words OFFICE OF PREDATOR AND PEST CONTROL stencilled on the opaque glass. Behind the door, past the defending secretary, I might find a fresh faced young fellow with a degree in wildlife biology, who would never dream of knocking on anyone's door and shyly offering to cure their land of prairie dogs.

The industrious young fellow might leave off shuffling important papers to hear my complaint. He might well decide to take the rare opportunity of meeting an actual taxpayer face to face to brag a bit about how efficiently the agency deals with pests and predators. He might even describe the cutting edge technology employed to protect us all.

"Mr. Quinlan," he might say, "if you will fill out these forms, those prairie dogs don't have a chance."

I hesitate to complain for fear this humorless fellow and his streamlined, technology-bloated agency might not understand the durable little joke and cure the land too hard.

The owls and eagles would starve out and move on. I would miss them and miss the excited barks of the silly little prairie dogs. Just as every year, along in May, I miss the knock of Placido Gardunio. ◆

MATES

You feel good
Most of the time;
Some days even like
The salty young buck
Who gathered the wildest cows
And relished flanking calves
To show crusty older hands
That you were not afraid of work,
Or dirt, or worse.

You got enough schooling
To understand how numbers work
And have lived long enough
To know how life begins,
Progresses, and ends.
Why then, are you so shocked
On this tired harvest morning,
To see nearly five decades
Etched plainly in the face
Of your mate.

Randy Everitt, Jerry Souza, and Ross Knox, Cowboy Bar, Montello, Nevada, photograph by Kurt Markus

WORKING MAN'S BARS

There are thousands in Colorado,
With names like THE SILVER SPUR,
THE MOTHER LODE, and THE BLUE OX;
I am comfortable in most
But, like any connoisseur, have favorites.
THE GOLDEN BURRO in Leadville,
HERB'S DOG HOUSE in Pueblo,
With its sign behind the bar
That warns, "man who spend too much time
In DOG HOUSE end up in cathouse,"
THE LONE CONE BAR in Norwood
With its exciting mix of loggers,
Mill-hands, bender bound sheepherders,
And an occasional delegation of volatile
Hardrock miners from Naturita,
The unpredictable BUCKET OF BLOOD in Silt,
And the world's greatest cowboy bar,
SAMMY'S WONDER BAR in Walsenburg.

It is fair to ask why a man
With a limited taste for alcohol
Should develop such an affection
For rowdy rough-neck bars
That his first draft poems
Are often written on Coors napkins,
Instead of yellow legal pads
Like a real poet.
Perhaps it's the gaudy jukebox
With Ol' Webb singing "Wondering"
In the old days and Ol' Willie singing
"The City of New Orleans" these days,
Or maybe a special fondness for men
That earn theirs with honest labor,
But mostly it's the rough charm of women
Who know how they inspire men
To climb all those mountains
And are too honest to pretend
It's all fried chicken and clean socks.

OVERLEAF: MC Ranch, Adel, Oregon, photograph by Kurt Markus

VESS QUINLAN

HENRY REAL BIRD

MONTANA

Henry Real Bird, photograph by Peter de Lory

Hank runs the O-W ranch in the Wolf Teeth Mountains of Montana. Unusually for so far north, his herd includes a number of longhorn cattle on Yellow Leggins Creek. He grew up speaking the Crow Indian language and, from an early age, decided to learn all he could about his native culture. A book of poetry, Where Shadows Are Born, *was published in 1990 and reprinted by the University of Findlay in 1992. Hank says that writing is as important to cowboying as is knowing the "rules and regs of the subsidies handbook," since the goal of both should be to maintain spiritual and ecological harmony. Hank also works as Registrar at Little Big Horn College in Crow Agency, Montana.* — CD TRACK 6

MY GRANDFATHER'S STORY

Years after hearing the creation story of the Crow people from his grandfather, Hank wrote the whole narration down, both as a pictograph (see page 57) and as a sixty-page English text. This excerpt tells how the Crow people came to live where they do, in their search for buffalo grass which their cattle thrive on today.

My grandfather wore three braids, one on each side of his head. His hair was braided loosely to cover his ears and the middle of the back of his head. His bangs were cut about even with the width of his head, greased down with buffalo fat, and combed straight back, which left his forehead bare with a scar clearly visible on the left side.

He was dressed as a white person in gray cotton and wore a black felt reservation hat with stampede strings and a small, round, brass-studded leather hatband so that his eyes would not be dazzled by the sunlight.

This is how he was dressed. But underneath all of the white clothing, he wore a breech cloth.

He always said that Old Man Coyote, the force that brings the wind and the water, is the Chief, or Man Who Is Good, of the People With a Breech Cloth – of all native Americans.

My grandfather was probably one of the last men ever to wear a breech cloth, even to the day he died. He used to say that he was one of the first Crow Indian children to go to school, to taste beef, and to drink the milk of a domesticated beef cow.

I led grandfather's horse, Painted Black, to the bank of the river as he stepped into the saddle from the uphill side. He wiggled into the saddle and evened his reins so as to motion me to get on behind him on Painted Black.

I threw my left leg over, got behind the cantle of the saddle, and hung on to his waist and pressed the left side of my face gently against his back.

We crossed the river, and he went upstream until he saw the fox's foot prints on the sandy edge of the Little Big Horn River. As we turned and went where the fox had gone, my grandfather, Owns Painted Horse, told me this story.

At one time, a long time ago, two girls were gathering firewood. As they were picking up dry cottonwood limbs that the wind had knocked down, they came upon a porcupine. When the porcupine saw the girls it didn't move. One of the girls said, "I need some quills to do some quill work. I'll go get some from that porcupine."

The girl who wanted the quills began to walk toward the porcupine, which started to walk, too. There the porcupine went, among the trees and bushes, wobbling slowly along. The girl began to run, so the porcupine moved faster. Finally the porcupine climbed a cottonwood tree and the girl turned back to her friend, and hesitated. She looked at her friend and thought for a few seconds, not saying a word as she stared into the right corners of her eyes.

She looked at her friend for a while longer, then walked to the cottonwood tree that the porcupine was on and started to climb. The porcupine didn't move as the girl climbed to get closer. When she got too close the porcupine would climb again. Higher and higher, with the girl right behind, the porcupine went up the tree.

The girl on the ground could see that the cottonwood tree which the porcupine and her friend were climbing was getting taller and taller and was going up into the clouds. The girl on the ground

Great Basin, watercolor by William Matthews

said, "Stop! I think the porcupine is taking you away. Something is wrong." But the girl in the tree could not hear a thing, and kept following the porcupine up the tree into the clouds.

When she climbed through the clouds and got on top of the clouds, the land looked just like the one that she had left. There were mountains, trees, flowers, birds, buffalos, elk, deer, flies and butterflies, and many other beautiful living things.

The porcupine that she followed turned into a man on this land above the clouds. She looked around and found the land beautiful. "It was the Sun that asked me to go after you. He wants to marry you," said the man that came out of the porcupine.

It is said that the Sun was a man with a face that is good. His braids were nice and neat. His necklace was a star so shiny and bright that he was hard to see.

The girl married the Sun. She was a good and beautiful woman who could tan hides and take good care of food. The Sun's teepee was great. The inside of the teepee was nice and neat with white and soft tanned hides. The teepee was beautiful and good. The Sun was a great man and his wife was a good woman, too.

She gave the Sun a good heart and she also had a good heart as the days and moons went by. They had plenty of dry meat, dry roots, dry berries, and plenty of good hides for clothing. They were living in goodness.

After the first winter and on the tenth moon that she was with the Sun, she gave birth to a boy. The Sun and his wife took care of their boy as the days, moons, and winters went by, blown by the wind of the four different grounds, in the land above the clouds in the sky.

When the Sun's little boy was four winters old, he had become very skilled in jumping and running around to play. He was like all children, going everywhere and thinking of nothing as he played. His father, the Sun, made him a bow and arrows to play with and taught him how to use them. His arrows were colored red, blue, green, and yellow.

The Sun, his wife, and his boy were doing good as life went on. There were some things the Sun didn't want his wife or his boy to do. He said to his wife, "Never dig for the big bunch turnip, and never turn over a buffalo chip." Then he said to his boy, "Never shoot the meadowlark with your bow and arrows."

They lived in goodness, but for some unknown reason the mother and her boy always felt like doing what they were told not to do. One day the little boy wanted to go digging for turnips. So his mother put him on her back and they went looking for turnips in the hills. As she began to dig for turnips, the boy started to play, as if he were a man going off on a war party. He would shoot his arrows all over the place, and then go after them. He would return to his mother and peel some turnips to eat them. This little boy would stay close, then wander off, then return.

The Sun's boy was using his bow and arrows when a meadowlark began playing around him. At first he tried not to see him because his father, the Sun, had told him not to shoot the meadowlark with his bow and arrows. The meadowlark would dive at him and almost hit him.

The boy finally got mad and shot an arrow at the meadowlark. He almost shot him good but just nicked him on the beak. The teasing meadowlark got mad, too, and said, "You're not one of us, you're a Crow boy. Go home. Your people are somewhere else." This made the little boy sad because he wasn't one of them. He always thought that he was one of the people of his father, the Sun.

And then the boy cried and ran to his mother to tell her what the meadowlark had said to him.

She thought of how her husband, the Sun, had warned her against digging the bunch turnip and turning over buffalo chips. Finally, she decided to go look for some bunch turnip and buffalo chips. It wasn't long before she found a buffalo chip on top of a bunch turnip. She went ahead and did what she was told not to do. With her deer horns, she flipped over the buffalo chip on top of the bunch turnip and saw a hole in the ground. She could look through the hole to see another ground below the one she was on. It was different and had a lot of people and teepees. The people were playing kick ball and they seemed to be having fun. The children were playing, too, and made a lot of noise.

Then suddenly, at that very moment, she remembered where she was from. She felt lonesome and missed her people and the land that she was from.

Then she and her boy went home, but it wasn't how it used to be. Both were sad that they had done what they had been told not to do.

When the Sun saw his wife and boy, he could tell that they were sad because their eyes were swollen from crying. The Sun said, "Both of you have done what I have told you not to do, and that's the reason you are sad." To his wife he said, "If you want to go back to your people, I'll send you and our boy back to where you came from."

And so the Sun told his hunters to go out and kill ten big buffalo bulls. With the sinew from these buffalos' backs, a spider spun a rope for the Sun. The Sun took his wife and son to the hole in the ground in the sky. Then he dropped the rope through the hole in the ground, above the clouds, and let it down. They could see the ground where the woman came from through the hole. She put her boy on her back and climbed down the buffalo sinew rope. The Sun's boy took with him the bow and arrows that his father, the Sun, had made for him. They got to the end of the rope, but they did not yet touch the ground and were hanging above a cotton-wood tree. The reason the rope was short was because the spider or one of the hunters took some of the sinew for their own use.

The woman was scared so she just hung on to the end of the rope and would not let go or jump to the ground where she had come from.

The Sun yelled, "Let go and jump!" But the woman would not jump and just held onto the rope. Finally, the Sun tied the rope to a sagebrush and went looking for a rock. Now, sagebrush have long roots that go deep into the ground and are very hard to pull out, which is why the Sun tied the buffalo sinew rope to the sagebrush. The Sun got a rock and covered it with buffalo wool so he could hit his wife on the head and she would drop back to the ground where she came from.

He said to the rock, "You can hit the woman on the head and kill her if you have to, but don't touch the boy." He then dropped the rock and hit his wife on the head.

The Sun's wife fell to the ground and died, but her little boy was all right. The little boy was so young, he didn't know that his mother had died. He would play and wander around by his mother. He didn't know anything, so he would always return to his dead mother. They fell to the ground right next to a garden. The little boy would go into the garden to eat some squash and corn and to play around.

The garden belonged to an old lady who wondered who it was that was eating her squash and corn and leaving little footprints behind. The little boy would take bites out of the squash and corn and would leave the garden in a mess. She knew it was a child that was eating the corn and squash. The old lady wanted to know whether this child was a boy or a girl. So one day she made a doll and a bow and arrows and placed them in her garden. The next day when the old lady returned, the bow and arrows were gone. There were arrow holes in some of her squash so she knew that it was a little boy.

"Little boy, I am alone. I want you to be my grandson, and I'll watch over you," said the old lady. Then there was a silence.

Finally, the little boy came out. He told where he had come from and how he came to be on this ground.

The old lady said, " You are my grandson. It was my daughter that climbed the tree after the porcupine."

My grandfather told the story, and when he was through we kept riding through the sagebrush on a trail going up a hill to the north of Medicine Tail Coulee. The willow whip that he had would tap Painted Black's right hind quarter and would keep perfect time with his walk. When we got on top the hill, he looked around and then began to talk again.

"This is all that's left of Crow's ground. Way over there, do you see where it is hot, toward that mountain? 'Mountain With Something Beyond' is the name of that mountain, and further down there are many more mountains and rivers. Where the sun sets, we once lived among many mountains. Go alongside that mountain, then go toward where it is cold. Mountain Chief is there," my grandfather said as he looked at the mountain.

"Before, we used to be near Mountain Chief, too. During winter, all the time. We come from there, they say. We have also lived where the sun rises, where the ground is flat. The first of our people comes from there. Where the sun comes out, and a little to the left, is where we are from.

"Once, we used to live in goodness. Old Man Coyote made four different grounds in the wind, and we would follow along to use the good in the wind. Now, the way the ground moves is different." We walked along the trail toward home through the sagebrush and back into the river bottom past buffalo berry bushes and stopped among cottonwood trees. The birds were chirping and whistling cheerfully with pride, dignity, and sweet innocence. A meadowlark flew at us, as in the story that my grandfather had told. We saw a flicker woodpecker, some hawks, sage hens, magpies, and a lone eagle circling above us in the big turquoise sky. There were many more birds as we approached an old river bed with still waters.

Then we heard the fluttering of wings as two waterbirds flew from the water going up stream toward Mountain With Something Beyond. Then, my grandfather and I returned to the Little Big Horn along old buffalo trails where horses and cattle now go to water. ◆

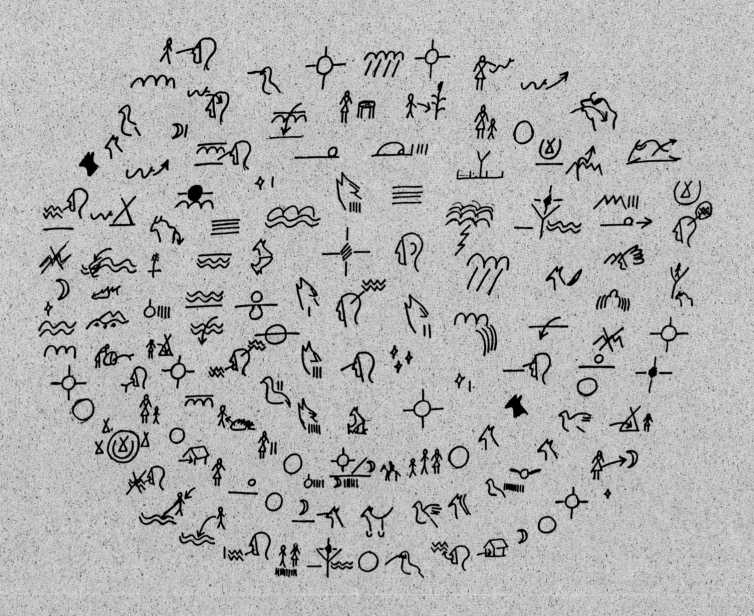

This pictograph is the visual transcription of the Crow creation story told to Henry Real Bird by his grandfather, Mark Real Bird. The story evolved over generations until Henry transcribed it by mixing ancient pictographs with his own. He now borrows from it when writing poetry. The story explains where thought comes from, what life is made of, and who the sun, the moon, and the star that is light are. The pictograph is read by beginning in the center with the gatekeeper figure (✦) and spiraling outwards in a clockwise movement to the Old Man Coyote (🐾) — who was asked by He Who Did Everything to remake the earth. Old Man Coyote taught the Crow people thought-ways (🐾). Wind is where Old Man Coyote comes from. Within the wind, say the Crow people, are contained many good things.

RED SCARF

Boots and jinks
Silver bit and silver spurs
Eased into the dawn
To walk out kinks
Horse like shiney, free of burrs
Trotted into day
I'm ridin' bay
If you can see the beauty
In the sunset with many colors
I only see the beauty
In the sunrise with many colors
You can find me
In the beauty in the sky
In sunrise and sunset
In the shadow of the sky
Among the stars
If you can see the beauty, in the sky
You can find me, in your eye
With a red scarf on
Boots and chinks
Here I am, I'm ridin' gone
Ground about day
Lookin' for a stray
Red tail hawk blessed me with his shadow
Clouds peak to my south
Granite to the west
Sheep Mountain and the Pryors
Look their best
Grass full grown
As I stood

In my heart that is good
If you can see the beauty
In the sunset with many colors
I only see the beauty
In the sunrise with many colors
You can find me
In the beauty in the sky
In sunrise and sunset
In the shadow of the sky
In the shadow of the sky
Among the stars

Red Scarf, watercolor by William Matthews

TAIL THAT'S LIGHT

Goin' on fresh snow
Snows been fallin'
Several days
The ground, all is white
Sagebrush tops
Stickin' out of snow
Ridin' through snow, it's quiet
River where it goes
Just the tress are black
The ground, all is white
Where there are pine trees
It's sorta blue, almost black
Still farther beyond
Wolf Teeth Mountains, pine trees are blue
There's nothing, but the cold wind
Look sort of like smoke
Ash trees, where they're thick
It is black
Gray I'm ridin'
His breath is white
Gray . . . Ground he is like this day
My song, I'm singin'
Lookin' around
Where the sun appears
Pink, peeps out of blue sky
Goin' to get many horses
Ridin' Gray, they won't see me
In white gray, blue black winter day
My song, I'm singin'

YP Ranch, Tuscarora, Nevada, photograph by Kurt Markus

LARRY SCHUTTE

NEVADA

Larry Schutte and his family, photograph by Kurt Markus

Larry Schutte has buckarooed on many of the large ranches of northern Nevada. He is accomplished at making intricate horsehair ropes (macartes), and recites and sings classic cowboy poems and songs with a voice that rings with the truth of first-hand experience. Originally from Twin Falls, Idaho, he, his wife, Toni, and their two children Riata and John, pictured above, have just moved from day cow work in Battle Mountain, Nevada, to leasing the Big Springs Ranch near Oasis, Nevada.

— CD TRACK 7

THAT LITTLE BLUE ROAN

There are many cowboy poems about favorite animals — horses, dogs, and even cows.
This well-known poem by Bruce Kiskaddon is a favorite of Larry Schutte.

Most all of you boys have rode hosses like that.
He wasn't too thin but he never got fat.
The old breed that had a moustache on the lip;
He was high at the wethers and low at the hip.
His ears always up, he had wicked bright eyes
And don't you furgit he was plenty cow wise.

His ears and his fets and his pasterns* was black
And a stripe of the same run the length of his back.
Cold mornin's he'd buck, and he allus would kick
No hoss fer a kid or a man that was sick.
But Lord what a bundle of muscle and bone;
A hoss fer a cow boy, that little blue roan.

For afternoon work or for handlin' a herd,
He could turn any thing but a lizard or bird.
For ropin' outside how that cuss could move out.
He was to 'em before they knowed what 'twas about.
And runnin' down hill didn't faize him aytall.
He was like a buck goat and he never did fall.

One day in the foot hills he give me a break
He saved me from makin' a awful mistake,
I was ridin' along at a slow easy pace,
Takin' stock of the critters that used in that place,
When I spied a big heifer without any brand.
How the boys ever missed her I don't onderstand.
Fer none of the stock in that country was wild,
It was like takin' candy away from a child.

She never knowed jest what I had on my mind
Till I bedded her down on the end of my twine.
I had wropped her toes up in an old hoggin' string*,
And was buildin' a fire to heat up my ring*.
I figgered you see I was there all alone
Till I happened to notice that little blue roan.

That hoss he was usin' his eyes and his ears
And I figgered right now there was somebody near.
He seemed to be watchin' a bunch of pinon,
And I shore took a hint from that little blue roan.

Instead of my brand, well, I run on another.
I used the same brand that was on the calf's mother.
I branded her right pulled her up by the tail
With a kick in the rump for to make the brute sail.
I had branded her proper and marked both her ears,
When out of the pinons two cow men appears.

They both turned the critter and got a good look
While I wrote the brand down in my old tally book.
There was nothin' to do so they rode up and spoke
And we all three set down fer a sociable smoke.
The one owned the critter I'd happened to brand,
He thanked me of course and we grinned and shook hands
Which he mightn't have done if he only had known
The warnin' I got from that little blue roan.

pasterns part of a horse's foot between the fetlock and hoof
hoggin' string a short rope used to hogtie calves
ring a portable branding iron

COWPEN MOO-SIC

When Larry recites this bovine sound poem by the late New Mexican poet,
S. Omar Barker, the nods of approving cowpunchers confirm that the poet really "got it right."

They asked me: "What's a beller?" Well, a beller is a bawl
That ain't exactly like a *moo* nor yet like a squall.
An ol' cow *moos* to coax her calf from close by in the brush.
She *bawls* all night at weanin' time, until you wish she'd hush.
But when she *bellers,* that's a sound that's got a heap more meanin'
Than just plain cowpen moo-sic that you hear when calves are weanin'.

For instance, let a range cow smell fresh blood from some dead critter —
It's then she sure 'nough *bellers* like she thinks all hell would git her.
Her tongue shoots out about a foot, and them weird sounds she makes
Sound terrible enough to give a man the chills and shakes.
Then all the cattle roundabout come snuffin' at a trot
To help her beller for the dead, and when they reach the spot,
There ain't no squall the banshee makes will make your neck hair rise
Like that there bovine blood call as it echoes to the skies
And if among the mourners some ol' bull joins in the tune,
'Twill purt near melt the marrow of the man up in the moon.
Of course, you know it's really just a harmless bovine sound,
But deep inside it shakes you like an earthquake shakes the ground.

Well, that's one kind of beller, and another that I'll name
Is two range bulls a-talkin' fight. Although it ain't the same,
It's also gizzard-stirrin' to a man with cowboy ears,
Who understands the language of the rangeland sounds he hears.
For though most plain steer bawlin' may be just a restless notion,
The sure 'nough beller is a sound of plumb raw cow emotion.

A calf may beller when he's roped or branded, and a cow
Will beller when she's on the prod. I better tell you how
To tell a beller from a bawl. It ain't alone the sound.
A bawl is mostly pointed up, a beller towards the ground;
And also, if on "beller facts" you're still somewhat in doubt,
A bawl becomes a beller when its tongue is stickin' out!

Heifers, photograph by Martin Schreiber

LINDA HASSELSTROM

SOUTH DAKOTA

Linda Hasselstrom, photograph by Peter de Lory

After moving to a South Dakota ranch at the age of nine, Linda began to explore the prairie, keep journals, and write fiction. Her feeling of closeness to the land was, if anything, intensified by returning to her native state after college and graduate school. Windbreak, her poetic diary from a year on the ranch, was followed by other books of essays and poetry including Land Circle: Writings Collected from the Land *in 1992 and the poetry volume* Dakota Bones *in 1993. One observer wrote of Linda, "She can deliver a calf and a poem on the same day — after mending a fence." Of her own work, she has written, "The work that occupies most of my time — writing and ranching — is complementary; physical and mental labor blend smoothly into a whole. I see my life as a circle: writing about, and laboring on, the land of the Great Plains."*

— CD TRACK 8

HANDBOOK TO RANCHING

Linda dedicated this poem to her rancher father.

Don't spend any money.

To conserve energy,
when a pickup is not moving ahead
shut the motor off.
Starters and batteries are cheaper
than gasoline these days.
Waste not, want not.

Don't keep horses in the corrals.
If there's snow on the ground
a horse can get by in a pasture without water.

Get the calves fed and watered before noon.
John Lindsay used to say
if he didn't get the work done in the morning,
he might as well go fishing the rest of the day.

Don't take chances. Don't get caught in a storm.
A cow can take more weather than you can.

Don't scatter thistles or cheat grass;
stack them in one pile and burn it.

Scatter hay in little bunches so each cow
or yearling can have one to itself;
they won't eat hay
after they lay on it.

Don't waste feed; know how much
you're feeding to every animal.
A penny saved is a penny earned.
Never call a veterinarian if you can avoid it.

You can never tell what a bobtail cow will do.

STAYING IN ONE PLACE

Riding fence last summer
I saw a meadowlark caught by one wing.
(My father saw one caught so, once;
in freeing it, taught me compassion.)
                                    He'd flown
futile circles around the wire, snapping bones.
Head folded on yellow breast,
he hung by one sinew, dead.

Gathering cattle in the fall
I rode that way again;
his yellow breast was bright as autumn air
or his own song.

I'm snowed in now, only a path
from the house to the cows in the corral.
Miles away he still hangs,
frost in his eyesockets
swinging in the wind.

I lie heavy in my bed alone, turning, turning,
seeing the house layered in drifts of snow
and dust and years and scraps of empty paper.
He should be light, light
bone and snowflake light.

LINDA HASSELSTROM

RANCHER ROULETTE

As an occupation, ranching is precarious in more ways than one. Here, Linda lists personal injuries
and those of friends, and ends the poem with a line discovered in a newspaper.

It's no trick to get killed ranching.
You might get a foot caught
in a stirrup when your horse bucks, get dragged
to death; that's what happened to my half brother.
He was riding that ridge to the south there;
his wife found him, after the storm.

Or tip the tractor over on a slope. Or forget
to turn off the power takeoff, and get your pants leg caught.
That happened to a neighbor, back in the forties.
By the time his kids saw the tractor circling,
he wasn't any bigger than a baseball.
Just wound him right around it.

Or you could get bit by a rattler, fixing fence.
I killed one with my shoe once, clean forgot
that left my foot sort of vulnerable.
Knew a fella ended up in a dam, drowned;
folks said he must have fell off his horse
and hit his head, but he was courting the daughter of a man
who didn't like him much.

A horse can kick you in the head;
you can get hit by a bull or stomped
by a cow that just calved. I got thrown from my horse
one time — well, more than that — but this one time
I was knocked out, and when I woke up
my head was between two rocks.
If I'd hit either one,
my head would have popped like a watermelon.

Knew a guy fell off the windmill once —
he was fixing it and the wind come up. Jammed his hips
up somewhere around his ears. I damn near drowned
trying to get a rope under a cow stuck in a mudhole.
She thrashed around and pushed me under.
I finally lassoed her head and drug her out that way.
She died anyway; broke her back.

Freezing to death would be easy. After I fell
in the creek chopping ice I damn near died
before I could get fifty feet to the pickup.
It makes a person wonder if there ain't some other way
to make a living. I heard the other day lightning
struck a fella's place on his fifty-fourth birthday,
killed fifty-four cows standing under a tree.

He said, "I hope I don't live to be a hundred;
I can't afford it."

OPPOSITE: Rick Bates, YP Ranch, Tuscarora, Nevada, photograph by Kurt Markus
OVERLEAF: Russell Ranches, Eureka, Nevada, photograph by Kurt Markus

ROD McQUEARY

NEVADA

Rod McQueary, photograph by Peter de Lory

Rod McQueary is a third-generation cattle rancher from the Ruby Valley in Nevada, traditional ranch country where cattle are sorted horseback and calves and colts are roped on both ends for branding. Rod's poetry has developed in two directions, one humorous (his poem about a young rancher who inherits a chicken farm is a comedy classic), the other serious. In the latter vein, Rod has taken cowboy poetry into entirely new areas of experience, so much so that the epithet "cowboy" sounds inaccurate. A Vietnam veteran, Rod lived with troubling dreams for two decades, until the poetic impulse led him to attempt to exorcise them in verse. In Blood Trails, published by Dry Crik Press in 1993, he and another Vietnam vet, Bill Jones, describe their odyssey to liberate themselves from a personal and collective trauma. This new vein of writing possesses an unnerving honesty and willingness to look reality squarely in the face, however painful.

— CD TRACK 9

FOR SORRELY

It was just business between us,
     He and I,
He was wild and untrusting,
I thought training horses was to crawl on them,
     and ride.
I would rope and choke him,
Then catch one hind foot and stretch it
So he couldn't kick.
Hook my cinch ring* with a wire, and
Away we'd go.
He didn't buck often, when he did
It was hard and quick and flat
He'd bawl and spin, trying to unload
The man he never liked
     and would not trust.
I never petted Sorrely,
It was beneath us both.
The best we ever had,
For a friendship,
Was an uneasy
Truce.

A couple Sorrely horse-trades and a dozen years later
Returning from some fall cow-work,
Four or five of us stopped for the
Mayhew field gate
Below the Connelly Corrals.
Buster, on a borrowed Sorrely, stepped off
To let us through.
As his right foot hit the ground,
He saw his left spur caught in his
Hobble buckle.*
He tried to step right back,
But half-way on, Sorrely blew.
They scattered the rest of us like deer.
Trying to keep a bay filly from hitting the fence,
I watch it all over my shoulder.
Buster, hatless, both hands on the mecate,*
Sliding, sitting half-up,
Kicking frantically at his trapped boot.
Sorrely stampeding, bent by the load
On the snaffle bit,* bawling and kicking
At the old enemy.

At that moment,
I learned a lot about
Training horses.

cinch ring a ring at the end of a girth used to hold a saddle on a horse's back
hobble buckle a buckle used to immobilize a horse by tying two feet together
mecate a horsehair rope
snaffle bit a bridle bit made of two pieces joined flexibly together

ROD McQUEARY

73

LIFE AND TIMES

When they ask of Life,
What will I say?
Can I describe time that swirls,
Flits with fickle castanets,
And disappears?
A shrinking, self-swallowing serpent?

Sometimes in spring
When ropes with eyes
Fly to heads and heels

The smokey celebration of
Surviving another winter
Buys the seven-way* and Bud

Dusty faces crack from laughing
Bloody hands pass Copenhagen*
Back and forth

No furtive glances hopefully
Caress snowless ridges
Today
The future is studiously ignored
For the intensity of
Now

Ground crew limps – unnoticed
Tomorrows hips and rope-arm
Shoulders
Get no second
Thought

If
By God
We are a primitive
Futureless band

At least we avoid
That flatland
Urban trap
Of measuring life
With
Time

seven-way a vaccine against seven diseases
Copenhagen a brand of chewing tobacco

IN LIKE A LION

She showed her true colors
In the Middle Field Gate.
Trying to get past me,
Pirouetting like a dancer
Sliding, leaping for an advantage
Finding none, she shuts her eyes
For the blind run to freedom.
My horse is fresh, he bashes her
Off the feed ground, into the deep snow,
              and knocks her down.
She never takes another willing step
Toward the corral.

Two hours later,
She still will not drive toward the barn,
And I am ashamed
To ask my lathered saddle horse
To drag her any farther.

I step down to retrieve my rope
From her sweaty, sullen neck.
For her nasty disposition, and
Seven dead calves in two
Miserable, freezing days,
I can't resist a "goodbye"
Kick in her ribs.
"Get up, you weak-hearted bitch."
She does.
A tussle erupts,
A mix of anger, exhaustion,
              and coils of rope.

That's what spooked my horse.

Currycomb, watercolor by William Matthews

J. B. ALLEN

TEXAS

J.B. Allen, photograph by Peter de Lory

J.B. Allen has worked as a cowboy and served as ranch foreman for over thirty years on spreads from the Great Divide to Fort Worth, Texas. He now lives near Whiteface, Texas, where he tends a herd of crossbred cows. With his deep knowledge of cowboy tradition, J.B. possesses one of the most original and authentic voices in cowboy poetry today. His spelling and style reflect the patterns of speech used on ranches and in cow camps. The capitalization is also part of the deal. His book, Water Gap Wisdom, *was published in 1990, and a tape of his recitations,* Kindred Spirits, *followed this. About his writing, J.B. recently said: "I don't spend any time on my poetry. If something comes to me I write it down, and if it don't, I don't worry about it." In recognition of the originality and depth of his writing, he was awarded the Wilbur S. Shepperson Cowboy Poetry Scholarship by the Western Folklife Center, Elko, Nevada, in 1993. His latest cassette,* Treasures, *was released by Caliche Publishing in 1993.*

— CD TRACK 10

MEMENTOES

There are times when a cowboy wakes up in the morning, all aches and pains, and suddenly
realizes he may be past the point of riding the "rough stock." This is what happened to J.B. not long ago.

THE HURTIN IN YOUR SHOULDERS
TAKES THE GLINT OUT OF YOUR EYE
WHEN THEM RAMBUNCTIOUS FOUR YEAR OLDS
COME TIPPY TOEIN BY.

THAT LEG THAT'S HELD TOGETHER
BY THEM BOLTS AND SILVER PLATE
DON'T TAKE TOO KINDLY, HITTIN POSTS
THAT'S HOLDIN UP THE GATE.

BUSTED THUMBS THAT HAVE NO STRENGTH
AND KNUCKLES BENT AND SORE
CAIN'T HOLD THE REINS TO KEEP HIS HEAD
WITH THAT OL HACKAMORE.*

THEM KNEES WON'T BEND AND CATCH THE STURP
TO LIGHTLY STEP ASTRIDE,
AND WIDOW WOMEN SHOW MORE GRACE
WITH PETTICOATS TO HIDE.

THOSE KNOTTY RIBS THAT'S SPRUNG A MITE
AND KIDNEYS FLOATIN LOOSE
ARE FOND REMINDERS OF THE WRECKS
THAT FINALLY COOKED YOUR GOOSE.

BUT MEN YOU'VE KNOWN AND HORSES RODE
ARE WORTH EACH ACHIN SPOT,
FOR CITY FOLK DON'T HAVE THE CHANCE
AT MEMORIES THAT YOU'VE GOT.

THE DANGER AND EXCITEMENT
DRAW A PUNCHER LIKE A FLAME,
WITH LIVES COOPED UP IN SETTLEMENTS
A BEIN WAY TOO TAME.

SO SAVE YOUR SILLY LAWS FOR FOLK
WITH MILDER DISPOSITION,
AND LET A FELLER HAVE A CHANCE
TO GIT IN THIS POSITION.

FOR LIVIN AIN'T JUST SLIPPIN BY
TILL NINETY TWO OR THREE,
WHILE GOVERMINT AND LAWYERS
HOLD YOU BACK FROM BEIN FREE.

hackamore a halter with reins and a noseband instead of a bit

SOWERS AND REAPERS

A YOUNG MAN'S STRENGTH, TO HIS SURPRISE,
IS ONE DAY JUST NOT THERE,
AND, LOOKIN IN THE MIRROR,
SEES THE GREY THAT'S IN HIS HAIR.

THE DAILY CARES AND TRIALS
MAKE THE PASSIN YEARS SEEM LONG,
BUT HINDSIGHT ALWAYS CONTRADICTS
AND PROVES THAT THINKIN WRONG.

OL "TIME" IS STILL THE MASTER,
AND IT WON'T ADMIT DEFEAT.
IT JUST KEEPS ON A COMIN
AND WON'T EVER SOUND RETREAT.

BELIEFS WE HOLD ARE WHAT LIVES ON
BEYOND THAT SIX FOOT GRAVE,
FOR OTHERS WATCH OUR EVER MOVE
TO SEE HOW WE BEHAVE.

WE'LL NOT GIT BY FOR VERY LONG
WITH WORDS THAT JUST DON'T FIT,
FOR HOW WE REALLY LEAD OUR LIVES
WON'T KEEP THAT LANTERN LIT.

THE BEACON OF OUR ACTIONS
WILL LIGHT THE PATH WE WALK,
OBSCURIN THAT SMALL LANTERN
THAT'S FED BY FANCY TALK.

WHILE CUSSIN OUT THE REFEREE,
OR YOUNGUNS ON THE FIELD,
JUST STOP AND THINK A MINUTE
ON THE CROPS THAT IT WILL YIELD.

YOU PROBLY WOULDN'T ROB A BANK
OR SOME BIG LIQUOR STORE,
BUT WAYS THAT PASS FOR BIZNESS
SOMETIMES CHEATS A FELLER MORE.

THIS WORLD WON'T GIT NO BETTER
'LESS WE CHANGE OUR WAY OF DOIN,
AND SET OUR STANDARDS HIGHER
THAN THE COURSE WE'VE BEEN PURSUIN.

THE GENERATIONS DOWN THE ROAD
MUST REAP WHAT WE HAVE SOWN,
AND "TIME" WILL JUDGE OUR PLANTIN JOB
BY WHAT WE NOW CONDONE.

OO Ranch, Seligman, Arizona, photograph by Kurt Markus

NEW TRAILS

*Many cowboys are hard-nosed individuals, unused to showing feelings. But now with all
the cowboy poetry gatherings, they are starting to share their emotions and head down new trails.*

HARD OLD SHELLS PROTECTIN FEELINS
LAY IN SHAMBLES AT OUR FEET
AS THE LANCETS PIERCED THE ARMOR
GROWN IMMUNE TO CLUB OR SLEET.

BUT THE FOE WAS DEEP WITHIN
WHERE NONE HAD PLANNED FOR SLY ATTACK
BY THE FORCES LYIN DORMANT
WHILE WE FIT A HORSE'S BACK.

BRONC OR MAVERICK POSED NO PROBLEMS,
HARD AND FAST OR DALLY WELT,*
BUT THE PHRASES SHARED AMONGST US
LENT TO ALL EMOTIONS FELT.

THIRTY–FORTY–FIFTY YEARS
WERE SWEPT AWAY ON VERSES PENNED,
LEAVIN NAKED NERVE ENDS THROBBIN
THAT NO POULTICE KNOWN CAN MEND.

FAR TOO LATE TO HEAL THE FORTRESS
NONE CAN CHOOSE WHERE FATE MAY LEAD.
NAUGHT TO DO BUT RIDE THE CREST
AND TEND THE WOUNDS THAT CRACK AND BLEED.

dally welt in Spanish, *dale vuelta;* when roping, to wrap the rope around the saddle horn

OPPOSITE: About Face, watercolor by William Matthews
OVERLEAF: YP Ranch, Tuscarora, Nevada, photograph by Kurt Markus

J.B.ALLEN

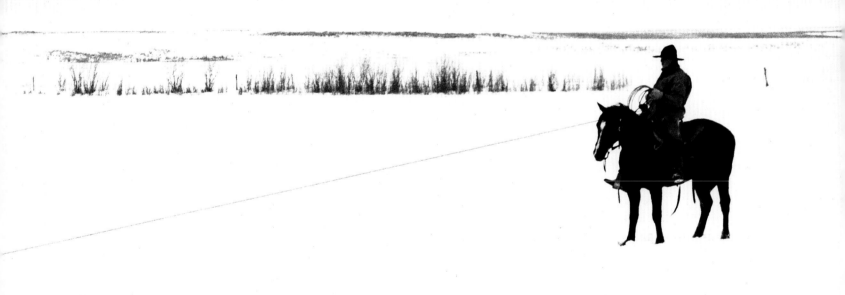

R.W. HAMPTON

NEW MEXICO

R.W. Hampton and his wife, Denise, photograph by Jay Dusard

R.W. Hampton has been ranching on high prairie country in northeastern New Mexico since 1985. A native of Texas, he started cowboying in Cimarron, New Mexico, at the age of sixteen — around the time he began to write music and poems. R.W. enjoys reading the work of Robert Service and Bruce Kiskaddon and listening to a favorite singer, Marty Robbins. A collection of his compositions entitled The One That I Never Could Ride was brought out by Adobe Records in 1991. As a way of keeping the cowboy spirit alive, R.W., along with his brother Jeff and David Marshall Marquis, recently created a one-cowboy musical entitled The Last Cowboy for the Loews Anatole Hotel in Dallas, Texas.   — CD TRACK 11

MY MARIA

*R.W. wrote this song while thinking one day of the joy he felt when
learning that a child was on the way to him and his wife, alias Maria.*

At the foot of the Sangre de Cristo's
There's a place where my heart longs to be,
The love light shines bright from the window
For all of the valley to see.
It's summer, the branding is over,
For three months I've been on the trail —
Boys, run in my horses tomorrow,
I'll ride like I'm carrying the mail . . .

Straight to Maria,
Warm as the soft summer wind that caresses the sage,
Brown-eyed Maria,
Every bird singing just seems to be calling your name,
I love you Maria,
Once in your sweet arms I never will leave you again.

I remember the day that we parted,
How she cried so when I rode away
Then whispered so soft and so sweetly
May "vaya con Dios," I pray.
Now the minutes have all seemed like hours,
The hours seem just like a day,
Counting the moments till I'll hold her again
And the words that I'm longing to say . . .

Oh my Maria,
Warm as the soft summer wind that caresses the sage,
Brown-eyed Maria,
Every bird singing just seems to be calling your name,
I love you Maria,
Once in your sweet arms I never will leave you again.

A week ago last Sunday morning
The boss brought a letter to me,
Sent by my dear wife Maria.
She said soon in our home there'll be three,
For the love that we shared in the springtime
Has bloomed like a rose in the sun,
The angels are bringing a baby to hold,
A love gift from heaven above.

I rode out the ranch gate at sunrise.
Left those hot dusty flats far behind.
Now on the high rolling prairie
Ridin' hard I can make it by night.
At the Rio I'll stop and swap horses,
Mounted fresh now I don't have far to go
To the valley of the Sangre de Cristo's
And the arms of the one I love so.

Oh my Maria,
Warm as the soft summer wind that caresses the sage,
Brown-eyed Maria,
Every bird singing just seems to be calling your name,
I love you Maria,
Once in your sweet arms I never will leave you again.

THE STREETS OF LAREDO

*This quintessential cowboy tune was first recorded as a shanty song in Ireland. Later it became
a seafarer's melody and then was adapted to the cowboy world. This version is sung by R.W. Hampton.*

As I walked out in the streets of Laredo,
As I walked out in Laredo one day,
I spied a young cowboy all wrapped in white linen,
All wrapped in white linen as cold as the clay.

"I see by your outfit that you are a cowboy,"
These words he did say as I slowly passed by.
"Come sit down beside me and hear my sad story
For I'm a young cowboy and I know I must die.

"Beat the drums slowly and play the fife lowly,
Play the dead march as you carry me along.
Down in the green valley there lay the sod o'er me,
I'm a young cowboy who's surely gone wrong.

"Go write a letter to my grey-headed mama
And go write the same to my sister as well,
But not a word of this will you mention
If someone should ask of my story to tell.

"There is another more dear than a sister,
She'll bitterly weep when she hears that I'm gone.
If some other cowboy should win her affection,
Don't mention my name and my name will pass on.

"Beat the drums slowly and play the fife lowly,
Play the dead march as you carry me along.
Down in the green valley there lay the sod o'er me,
I'm a young cowboy who's surely gone wrong.

"Get six pretty maidens to carry my coffin,
Get six jolly cowboys to bear up my pall.
Put bunches of roses all over my coffin
To deaden the sound of the clods as they fall.

"Go fetch me a cup of cool, cool water,
Go fetch a cup," then the dying cowboy said.
But when I returned his soul had departed,
Gone on to his Maker, the cowboy was dead.

Beat the drums slowly and play the fife lowly,
And play the dead march as you carry me along
Down in the green valley there lay the sod o'er me,
I'm a young cowboy who's surely gone wrong.

Bell Ranch, New Mexico, photograph by Martin Schreiber

OVERLEAF: Branding, Bell Ranch, New Mexico, photograph by Martin Schreiber

PAUL ZARZYSKI

MONTANA

Paul Zarzyski, photograph by Jay Dusard

"The stork dropped me in the wrong place," says Paul, who was born in Wisconsin but moved at an early age to Montana. Bitten by the rodeo bug, he rode bareback broncs for more than a decade, and for eight years as a member of the Professional Rodeo Cowboys Association. Now, Paul rides the poetry trail. "Whereas I once lived for the jump-'n'-kick, rock-'n'-rowel buckin' horse, I live now for the jump-'n'-kick, rock-'n'-rowel buckin' verse — the ring and ricochet of lingo off the stirrup bone of the middle ear. But I've never made a living at either." For years a noted proponent of innovative verse forms, Paul has taken the language of cowboy poetry into a new sphere. Some of the results can be seen in his collection, Roughstock Sonnets *(The Lowell Press, Kansas City, 1989), and heard in performances with the group Horse Sense, with whom Paul mixes cowboy music and poetry in new ways. Their album,* Ain't No Life After Rodeo, *appeared in 1992.* — CD TRACK 12

AIN'T NO LIFE AFTER RODEO

There ain't no life after rodeo.
Sulled-up old cowboys will tell you so.

So when you feel your spur-lick weaken,
And your bareback riggin' goes to leakin',

Bury your gripper elbow-deep,
To hell with looking before you leap!

Fight for those holts, sight down that mane,
Spit in the face of age and pain,

Give that hammerhead a hardware bath,
Dazzle the judges with '90's math,

Spur the rivets off your Wranglers,
A cappella rowels don't need "danglers,"

Rake like a maniac, tick for tick,
Tip your Resistol,* flick the crowd's Bic,

Fast-feet-fast-feet, gas-it-and-mash,
Toes turned out with each jab and slash,

Insanity, love, plus aggression,
Call it passion, call it obsession,

Adrenalined fury, 200 proof,
Like guzzling moonshine up on the roof,

Running on Bute*, LeDoux* songs and caffeine,
You rollicking, rosined-up, spurring machine,

Too lazy to work, too scared to steal,
Slaving for wages bushwhacks your zeal,

So charge that front-end for those 8,
You ain't no rodeo reprobate!

Grit each stroke out with every tooth,
Swimming the cowBOY fountain of youth,

Love that sunfish and love that high-dive,
BELIEVE you will ride till you're 95.

Resistol brand name of a cowboy hat
Bute an anti-inflammatory drug used by some bronc riders
LeDoux Chris LeDoux, a cowboy singer and former world champ rodeo hand

PAUL ZARZYSKI

Rodeo, Clovis, California, photograph by Norman Mauskopf

THE BUCKING HORSE MOON

A kiss for luck, then we'd let 'er buck —
I'd spur electric on adrenaline and lust.
　　She'd figure-8 those barrels
on her Crimson Missile sorrel —
　　we'd make the night air swirl with hair and dust.

At some sagebrushed wayside, 3 a.m.,
we'd water, grain, and ground-tie Missile.
　　Zip our sleeping bags together,
make love in any weather,
　　amid the cactus, rattlers, and thistle.

Seems the moon was always full for us —
it's high-diving shadow kicking hard.
　　We'd play kid games on the big night sky,
she'd say "that bronco's Blue-Tail Fly,
　　and ain't that ol' J.T. spurrin' off its stars?"

We knew sweet youth's no easy keeper.
It's spent like winnings, all too soon.
　　So we'd revel every minute
in the music of our Buick
　　running smooth, two rodeoin' lovers
cruising to another —
　　beneath Montana's blue roan
bucking horse moon.

The Augusta perf* at 2, we'd place again,
then sneak off to our secret Dearborn River spot.
　　We'd take some chips and beer and cheese,
skinny-dip, dry off in the breeze,
　　build a fire, fry the trout we caught.

Down moonlit gravel back to blacktop,
she'd laugh and kill those beams for fun.
　　That old wagon road was ours to own —
30 shows since I'd been thrown
　　and 87 barrels since she'd tipped one.

We knew that youth won't keep for rainy days.
It burns and turns to ash too soon.
　　So we'd revel every minute
in the music of our Buick
　　running smooth, two rodeoin' lovers
cruising to another —
　　beneath Montana's blue roan
bucking horse moon.

Augusta perf the rodeo performance in Augusta, Montana

PAUL ZARZYSKI

WALLACE McRAE

MONTANA

Wallace McRae, photograph by Peter de Lory

A rancher with a thirty thousand-acre cow-calf operation near Forsyth, Montana, Wally began writing poetry more than twenty-five years ago in an effort to record the values and qualities of his occupation. The author of four volumes of poetry, he became well known outside ranching circles thanks to a syndicated television program, "The West," on which he recited his verse regularly for two years. Wally has given cowboy poetry a richness and a subtlety that come across on the printed page as well as in his memorable recitations. In 1990 he became the first cowboy poet to be granted a National Heritage Fellowship from the National Endowment for the Arts in Washington, D.C. His most recent book, Cowboy Curmudgeon, was published by Gibbs Smith, Salt Lake City, in 1992.   — CD TRACK 13

THINGS OF INTRINSIC WORTH

Wally's ranch is located near a large coal strip mine, the development of which has transformed the landscape.

Remember that sandrock on Emmells Crick
Where Dad carved his name in 'thirteen?
It's been blasted down into rubble
And interred by their dragline machine.
Where Fadhls lived, at the old Milar place,
Where us kids stole melons at night?
They 'dozed it up in a funeral pyre
Then torched it. It's gone alright.
The "C" on the hill, and the water tanks
Are now classified "reclaimed land."
They're thinking of building a golf course
Out there, so I understand.
The old Egan homestead's an ash pond
That they say is eighty feet deep.
The branding corral at the Douglas camp
Is underneath a spoil heap.
And across the crick is a tipple, now,

Where they load coal onto a train.
The Mae West Rock on Hay Coulee?
Just black-and-white snapshots remain.
There's a railroad loop and a coal storage shed
Where the bison kill site used to be.
The Guy place is gone; Ambrose's, too.
Beulah Farley's a ranch refugee.

But things are booming. We've got this new school
That's envied across the whole state.
When folks up and ask, "How's things goin' down there?"
I grin like a fool and say, "Great!"
Great God, how we're doin! We're rollin' in dough,
As they tear and they ravage The Earth.
And nobody knows . . . or nobody cares . . .
About things of intrinsic worth.

MAGGIE

I taught my good dog, Maggie,
"Lay down," when I commanded.
I also taught her "Set,"
Whenever I demanded.

"I'll teach her now to speak," said I.
She labored to comply.
And when she learned to speak she said,
"You twit, it's 'sit' and 'lie!' "

Randy Reiman, watercolor by William Matthews

HAT ETIQUETTE

There are rules of decorum and conduct
    to which genuine cowboys attest.
Call them mores, traditions or manners,
    they're part of the code of the West.
But cowpokes have got this dilemma,
    that confuses these sage diplomats.
It involves the whens and when-not-tos,
    concerning the wearing of hats.
The old rule concerning head covers says
    "Hat-up when you work, or you ride.
Tip 'em to women. But take John B. off
    when in bed, or when you're inside."
But whaddya do in a gin mill,
    bean shops or dances in town?

Where Resistol rustlers'll filch it
    or some low-life'll puke in its crown.
'N there ain't no such thing as a hat rack
    anyplace that I been of late.
So we all compromise with a tip back,
    baring pallid foreheads and bald pate.
What we needs is a new resolution
    to settle this conflict we got.
So I come up with this here solution,
    a result of consider'ble thought:
"I move that we do like good Hebrews,
    wear hats from our birth 'til we die.
And never remove them sombreros.
All those in favor say, 'Aye.' "

LITTLE THINGS

I've laid for hours upon my back
Just looking at the sky,
At clouds, or if the sky was clear,
The motes within my eye.
D'ja ever spend an hour or more
Just staring at the crick?
Or a scarab roll a ball of dung?
Or ants rasslin' with a stick?
Or, on a cloudy, windy day,
See a windmill seem to fall?
Or stop stock still with neck hairs raised
By a plaintive coyote call?
Swallows slice their swaths across
The sky like scimitars.
I'm humbled by the intricate
Snowflakes' prismic stars.
I've laughed as stove-up killdeer
Go a-scrabblin' 'cross a draw.

I've seen cedar trees explode in flames
As I'm consumed with awe.
Arms crossed and leaning forward
Weight on the saddle horn,
I'm a fascinated crowd of one;
A calf is being born.

The measure of your intellect,
The learn-ed people say,
Are the things that fascinate us.
They're a mental exposé.
You got to be dang careful
If you want to be thought smart,
And keep sorta confidential
Little things that's in your heart.

E.M. (RED) KLUVER

What sort of a man was the Red Pup, you say?
Hard, Oh Lord, he was hard.
And how did he go? Did he just slip away?
Hard, No Lord, he died hard.

And how did he live? Was he easy and free?
Hard, Oh Lord, he lived hard.
Now in the big war, did he cower and flee?
Hard, No Lord, he fought hard.

He used to ride broncs. Did he have the knack?
Hard, Oh Lord, he rode hard.
And how did he work? Did he kinda lay back?
Hard, Oh Lord, he worked hard.

What of his looks? Was he attractively made?
Hard, Oh Lord, he looked hard.
What of his values? Was he easily swayed?
Hard, No Lord, he was hard.

Not soft then, or wavering? You'd say in its stead . . .
Hard, Oh Lord, he was hard.
And how do you feel, now that he's dead?
Hard, Oh Lord, it's so hard.

MY REQUIEM

Some leave their mark on a branded hide.
Some on the furrowed earth.
Some aspire to reproduce
Themselves in those they birth.
Some leave their marks on canvas,
Bronze or stone that will survive.
Long after their creator
No longer is alive.

Some would build an edifice,
An architectural gem,
To serve throughout the ages
As a lasting requiem.
But grant to me this final wish
When I say that last amen:
Let my mark be carried lightly
In the hearts and minds of men.

Big Springs Ranch, Bruneau, Idaho, photograph by Kurt Markus

Ricky Morris and Hank Brackenberry, IL Ranch, Nevada, photograph by William Albert Allard

IAN TYSON

ALBERTA, CANADA

Ian Tyson, photograph by Jay Dusard

Ian's musical career now spans more than thirty years and has produced such classic cowboy albums as Cowboyography, And Stood There Amazed, *and* I Outgrew the Wagon. *A native of British Columbia, he was nurtured on his father's passion for the cowboy as well as the books of Will James. After high school rodeoing, logging, and construction jobs, Ian learned to play guitar while recovering from a rodeo accident. In 1958 he hitch-hiked to Toronto and found work as a graphic artist, and played in the emerging folk club circuit. By 1961 he was singing with Sylvia Fricker and created a unique vocal style which is reflected in famous songs such as "Four Strong Winds" and "Someday Soon." In the 1970s Ian bought a one hundred sixty-acre ranch in the foothills of the Rockies, outside Longview, Alberta, where he pursued his boyhood cowboying dream and began to raise cutting horses. Perhaps more than any living singer-songwriter, Ian embodies the cowboy perspective, which songs like "Summer Wages," "Cowboy Pride," and "The Gift" have helped to commemorate.*

— CD TRACK 14

FIFTY YEARS AGO

If I could roll back the years
Back when I was young and limber
Loose as ashes in the wind
I had no irons in the fire
I could ride them wild young broncos
The adrenaline came quickly
And Juanita down at Mona's
Was my only heart's desire

We were living for the moment
And the sunlight on my silver bits
The ringing of my jinglebobs
Was the music of my soul
In the alley back of Mona's
I held Juanita in the shadows
How we held on to each other
And the lovin' that we stole

CHORUS:
And the sighing of the pines
Up here near the timberline
Makes me wish I'd done things different
But wishing don't make it so
Oh the time has passed so quick
The years all run together now
Did I hold Juanita yesterday
Was it fifty years ago

If I would have quit them broncos
She might have quit that business
But that was back in the fast days
You know before the wire
I bet I could still find her
Bet she's still as pretty
As when she's Juanita down at Mona's
And my only heart's desire

REPEAT CHORUS TWICE

ZX Ranch, Paisley, Oregon, photograph by Kurt Markus

SPRINGTIME

Bald eagles back in the cottonwood tree
The old brown hills are just about bare
Springtime sighing all along the creek
Magpies ganging up everywhere
Sun shines warm on the eastern slope
March came in like a lamb for a change
Gary's pulling calves at the old stampede
We made it through another on the northern range
Lonnie's pulling calves at the top of the world
We made it through another on the northern range

Well the big chinook blew in last week
Warm and strong from the western sea
Pretty soon water running everywhere
Hell, it couldn't run fast enough for me
Broodmare's sleeping in the afternoon sun
She's shedding hair everywhere
Time for a change
George's pulling calves at the T-Y
We made it through another on the northern range
Waddie's pulling calves at the Little E
We made it through another on the northern range

Bald eagles back in the cottonwood tree
The old brown hills are just about bare
Springtime sighing all along the creek
Magpies ganging up everywhere
Sun shines warm on the eastern slope
March came in like a lamb for a change
Larry's pulling calves at the Quarter Circle S
We made it through another on the northern range
Allan's pulling calves at the Bar 4 Oarlock
We made it through another on the northern range
Jean's pulling calves at the Horseshoe Bar
We made it through another on the northern range
Ian's in the hills trying to write songs
Gid's in the country where the tall grass grows

Gray Ranch, New Mexico, photograph by Jay Dusard

OVERLEAF: Whitehorse Ranch, Fields, Oregon, photograph by Kurt Markus

WADDIE MITCHELL

NEVADA

Waddie Mitchell and his son, Chaz, photograph by Kurt Markus

Waddie has cowboyed for most of his life and was for years ranch boss on a spread between Lee and Jiggs, Nevada. If the American public knows a cowboy poet and reciter, it is likely to be Waddie since he has made several appearances on national television. Waddie is best known for his recitations of the classic poems of the cowboy tradition, but his own poetry is gaining attention in books and national periodicals. He grew up on his father's ranch and vowed one day he would have his own spread. After working as a buckaroo, he settled down, had five children, and worked his way up managing ranches. Realizing that his dream of owning his own ranch will never happen on cowboy wages, Waddie now spends much of the year promoting the cowboy movement in appearances around the country. Currently signed with Warner Western Records, Waddie has helped launch the new record label with an album of recitations entitled Lone Driftin' Rider *in 1992, which was followed by* Buckaroo Poet *in 1993.*

— CD TRACK 15

WHAT WILL I TELL HIM?

"When I was sixteen," Waddie remembers, "I just didn't think I was needin' school anymore.
When my boy was gonna turn sixteen, I was asked, 'What are you gonna tell him if he comes up to you and says
that he's just gonna quit school, just go cowboy for a living?' So I thought about that."

What will I tell him, you ask me,
When my son's trying to make up his mind
To ride for a living like I have
Or explore what the world has to find.
Could I tell him it's sure worth the doing?
Could I tell him I spent well my time?
I'll just say from the start,
Son, it's gotta come from the heart,
It ain't something that comes from the mind.
I'll tell him the truth as I know it —
Of good years, hard winters, and drought.
The ecstasy of winnin' a round now and then
Givin' courage to stay in the bout.
That adrenaline rush when you're bustin' up brush
On a cowpony agile and stout,
Of having the rug jerked from under your feet

When you hear that the outfit sold out.
I'll tell him that cowboy's a verb not a noun;
It's what you do more than a name.
And he'd be foolin' himself if he's figurin'
On any sort of material gain.
I'll remind him of spring calves a buckin',
Of the joy and the pride and the pain
Of livin' a life that is easy or hard
At the discretion of nature's refrain.
What will I tell him, you ask me,
When he's there and tryin' to make up his mind?
I'll just say from the start,
Son, it's gotta come from the heart,
It ain't something that comes from the mind.

Heading Up to French Glen, watercolor by William Matthews

THE OLD NIGHT HAWK

This contemplative classic by Bruce Kiskaddon is one of Waddie's favorite poems to recite.

I am up tonight in the pinnacles bold
Where the rim towers high.
Where the air is clear and the wind blows cold,
And there's only the horses and I.
The valley swims like a silver sea
In the light of the big full moon,
And strong and clear there comes to me
The lilt of the first guard's tune.

The fire at camp is burning bright,
Cook's got more wood than he needs.
They'll be telling some windy tales tonight
Of races and big stampedes.
I'm gettin' too old fer that line of talk.
The desperaders they've knowed,
Their wonderful methods of handling stock,
And the fellers they've seen get throwed.

I guess I'm a dog that's had his day,
Though I still am quick and strong.
My hair and my beard have both turned grey,
And I reckon I've lived too long.
None of 'em know me but that old cook, Ed,
And never a word he'll say.
My story will stick in his old grey head
Till the break of the Judgement Day.

What's that I see a walkin' fast?
It's a hoss a slippin' through.
He was tryin' to make it out through the pass;
Come mighty near doin' it too.
Git back there! What are you tryin' to do?
You hadn't a chance to bolt.
Old boy I was wranglin' a bunch like you
Before you was even a colt.

It's later now. The guard has changed.
One voice is clear and strong.
He's singin' a tune of the old time range –
I always did like that song.
It takes me back to when I was young
And the memories came through my head,
Of the times I have heard that old song sung
By voices now long since dead.

I have traveled better than half my trail.
I am well down the further slope.
I have seen my dreams and ambitions fail,
And memory replaces hope.
It must be true, fer I've heard it said,
That only the good die young.
The tough old cusses like me and Ed
Must stay till the last dog's hung.

I used to shrink when I thought of the past
And some of the things I have known.
I took to drink, but now at last,
I'd far rather be alone.
It's strange how quick that a night goes by,
Fir I live in the days of old.
Up here where there's only the hosses and I;
Up in the pinnacles bold.

The two short years that I ceased to roam,
And I led a contented life.
Then trouble came and I left my home,
And I never have heard of my wife.
The years that I spent in a prison cell
When I went by another name;
For life is a mixture of Heaven and Hell
To a feller that plays the game.

They'd better lay off of that wrangler kid
They've give him about enough.
He looks like a pardner of mine once did.
He's the kind that a man can't bluff.
They'll find that they are making a big mistake
If they once git him overhet;
And they'll give him as good as an even break,
Or I'm takin' a hand, you bet.

Look, there in the East is the Mornin' Star.
It shines with a firy glow,
Till it looks like the end of a big cigar,
But it hasn't got far to go.
Just like the people that make a flash.
They don't stand much of a run.
Come bustin' in with a sweep and dash
When most of the work is done.

I can see the East is gettin' gray.
I'll gather the hosses soon;
And faint from the valley far away
Comes the drone of the last guard's tune.
Yes, life is just like the night-herd's song,
As the long years come and go.
You start with a swing that is free and strong,
And finish up tired and slow.

I reckon the hosses all are here.
I can see that T-bar blue,
And the buckskin hoss with the one split ear;
I've got 'em all. Ninety two.
Just listen to how they roll the rocks —
These sure are rough old trails.
But then, if they can't slide down on their hocks,
They can coast along on their tails.

The Wrangler Kid is out with his rope,
He seldom misses a throw.
Will he make a cow hand? Well I hope,
If they give him half a show.
They are throwin' the rope corral around,
The hosses crowd in like sheep.
I reckon I'll swaller my breakfast down
And try to furgit and sleep.

Yes, I've lived my life and I've took a chance,
Regardless of law or vow.
I've played the game and I've had my dance,
And I'm payin' the fiddler now.

OVERLEAF: IL Ranch, Tuscarora, Nevada, photograph by Kurt Markus

WADDIE MITCHELL

DON EDWARDS

TEXAS

Don Edwards, photograph courtesy of Warner Western Records

*One of the country's foremost exponents of traditional cowboy music, Don has per-
formed throughout the United States, Europe, and New Zealand during the last thirty
years. After chasing the rodeo and working on ranches in Texas and New Mexico, he
settled into a music career characterized as much by its distance from mainstream country music as its adherence to traditional cowboy music and cowboy swing. Don became
part-owner of the White Elephant Saloon in Fort Worth where he also played music. "A
lot of times I thought about giving it up," he reminisces. "I wasn't much for going with
the flow." Only after recording five albums was his passion for traditional cowboy song
vindicated by a major recording company. His album,* Songs of the Trail, *helped to
launch the new Warner Western Records label in 1992. A second album,* Goin' Back
to Texas, *appeared in 1993.* — CD TRACK 16

LITTLE JOE, THE WRANGLER

Composed by Nathan Howard "Jack" Thorp in 1898, and first sung by him in Johnny Roots's Saloon in Weed,
New Mexico, "Little Joe" is one of the most popular cowboy songs ever written. This version is sung by Don Edwards.

Now Little Joe, the wrangler, he'll wrangle never more;
His days with the remuda* they are o'er.
'Twas a year ago last April when he rode into our camp,
Just a little Texas stray and all alone.

'Twas late in the evening when he rode up to the herd
On a little old brown pony he called Chaw;
And with brogan shoes and overalls a tougher looking kid
You never in your life had ever saw.

Now his saddle was a Texas kack* built many years ago,
And an O.K. spur on one foot idly hung,
With his hot roll* in a cotton sack loosely tied behind
And a canteen from his saddle horn he'd slung.

Now he said he'd had to leave his home, his pa' married twice
And his new ma' whipped him every day or two;
So he saddled up old Chaw one night and lit a shuck* this way.
Now he's trying hard to paddle his own canoe.

Said he'd try and do the best he could if we'd only give him work
Though he didn't know straight up about a cow,
So the boss he cut him out a mount and kindly put him on
For he sorter liked the little kid somehow.

Now he learned to jingle horses and to learn them one and all
To round 'em up by daybreak if he could,
To follow the chuck wagon and to always hitch the team
And help the cosinero* rustle wood.

Now we'd driven to Red River the weather being fine;
We were camped down on the south side in a bend
When a norther commenced blowing and we doubled up our guards
For it took all hands to hold the cattle in.

Little Joe the wrangler, he was called out with the rest
And scarcely had the kid reached the herd
When the cattle they stampeded, like a hail storm, long they flew
And we were all riding for the lead.

Now midst the streaks of lightning we could see a horse far out ahead,
'Twas little Joe, the wrangler, in the lead;
He was riding old Blue Rocket with a slicker o'er his head,
Trying to check the leaders in their speed.

Now we finally got them milling and kinder quieted down
And the extra guard back to the wagon rode
But there was one a-missin' and we all knew at a glance
'Twas our little Texas stray, poor wrangler Joe.

Next morning just at sunup we found where Rocket fell
Down in a washout twenty feet below
And beneath his horse mashed to a pulp his horse had rung the knell
Was our little Texas stray, poor wrangler Joe.

Now Little Joe the wrangler, he'll wrangle never more;
His days with the remuda they are o'er.
Was a year ago last April when he rode into our camp,
Just a little Texas stray and all alone.

remuda a herd of saddle horses
kack another word for saddle
hot roll sleeping bag
lit a shuck perhaps lit a lantern using a shuck of corn so as to see through the dark
cosinero Spanish, *cocinero*, cook

Late in the Day, watercolor by Wiliam Matthews

Skeeter Clark, ZX Ranch, Paisley, Oregon, photograph by Kurt Markus

THE OLD COW MAN

The author of this poem, Charles Badger Clark, is one of the classic cowboy poets. Don had been reciting this work until one night he awoke from a dead sleep with an entire melody for it in his head. He put it down on a machine and recorded it professionally. Until then he had only heard people talk of this sort of experience.

I rode across a valley range
    I hadn't seen for years.
The trail was all so spoilt and strange
    It nearly fetched the tears.
I had to let ten fences down
    (The fussy lanes ran wrong)
And each new line would make me frown
    And hum a mournin' song.

Oh, it's squeak! squeak! squeak!
    Hear 'em stretchin' of the wire!
The nester brand is on the land;
    I reckon I'll retire,
While progress toots her brassy horn
    And makes her motor buzz,
I thank the Lord I wasn't born
    No later than I was.

'Twas good to live when all the sod,
    Without no fence nor fuss,
Belonged in pardnership to God,
    The Gover'ment and us.
With skyline bounds from east to west
    And room to go and come,
I loved my fellow man the best
    When he was scattered some.

Oh, it's squeak! squeak! squeak!
    Close and closer cramps the wire.
There's hardly play to back away
    And call a man a liar.
Their house has locks on every door;
    Their land is in a crate.
These ain't the plains of God no more,
    They're only real estate.

There's land where yet no ditchers dig
    Nor cranks experiment;
It's only lovely, free and big
    And isn't worth a cent.
I pray that them who come to spoil
    May wait till I am dead
Before they foul that blessed soil
    With fence and cabbage head.

Yet it's squeak! squeak! squeak!
    Far and farther crawls the wire.
To crowd and pinch another inch
    Is all their heart's desire.
The world is overstocked with men
    And some will see the day
When each must keep his little pen,
    But I'll be far away.

When my soul hunts range and rest
    Beyond the last divide,
Just plant me in some stretch of West
    That's sunny, lone and wide.
Let cattle rub my tombstone down
    And coyotes mourn their kin,
Let hawses paw and tromp the moun'
    But don't you fence it in!

Oh, it's squeak! squeak! squeak!
    And they pen the land with wire.
They figure fence and copper cents
    Where we laughed 'round the fire.
Job cussed his birthday, night and morn,
    In his old land of Uz,
But I'm glad I wasn't born
    no later than I was!

DON EDWARDS

A GUIDE FOR LISTENERS

The men and women featured in this book all come from ranching country and from the ranching life. Although they do not all live in the "buckaroo country" of Nevada, Oregon, Idaho, and California, these poets, singers, reciters, and storytellers have in common the fact that ranching and rural life is their most prominent cultural identification. What you hear on this compact disc has more to do with a T-bone steak than with recording contracts. Importantly, much of what is printed in the book was composed to be listened to, to be spoken or sung, not to be read. For this reason, the CD plays a special role in bringing the listener into contact with an essentially oral culture, where the campfire gathering is never too far away, in fact, in memory, or in fancy.

— Hal Cannon

CD SELECTIONS

All selections are performed by authors unless noted

1
JACK WALTHER: Lamoille, Nevada. "Defining the Buckaroo." Recorded by Hal Cannon, April 1993. 1:27

— PAGE 12

2
BUCK RAMSEY: Amarillo, Texas. "Git Along Little Dogies" (traditional). From the Wrangler Award-winning album, *Rolling Uphill from Texas*, on the Fiel Publications, Inc. label. This plaintive traveling song is an old standard from the trail-herding days of the mid-nineteenth century when young cowboys often felt like orphan dogies (motherless calves) on lonely trails. 3:02

— PAGE 16

3
SUNNY HANCOCK: Lakeview, Oregon. "A Bear Tale." Tall tales are a traditional way in which cowboys deal with stressful situations. Here, Sunny casts an amusing look at animal rights versus human rights. Recorded at the 1991 Cowboy Poetry Gathering, Elko, Nevada. 5:08

— PAGE 28

4
TERESA JORDAN: Iron Mountain, Wyoming, now based in Starr Valley, Nevada. "My Great-aunt Marie" and "My o dere children, I wish you were heare." A memoir of a great-aunt Teresa knew while growing up in southeastern Wyoming is followed by a poem inspired by letters sent by Abigail Malick to her family in the States after arriving in Oregon Territory in 1850, published in 1989 as *Far From Home: Families of the Westward Journey*, by Lillian Schlissel, Byrd Gibbens, and Elizabeth Hampsten, Schocken Books (see page 41). Recorded by Hal Cannon, May 1993. 2:20

— PAGE 36

5
VESS QUINLAN: Alamosa, Colorado. "Passing the Mantle" and "Soul of a Cowman." One-quarter of all American farmers or ranchers have moved away from the country during the past ten years. This fact underlies the concern ranching communities have for keeping continuity between generations. Recorded at the 1992 Cowboy Poetry Gathering, Elko, Nevada. 5:46

— PAGE 46

6
HENRY REAL BIRD: Garryowen, Montana. "So Sincerely Yours." Cowboys chant yippi-ti-yi-yay or they yodel. Indian cowboys sing traditional chants with English words in what are called "forty-nine songs." In both cases the gait of a horse provides the rhythm. Recorded at the 1993 Cowboy Poetry Gathering, Elko, Nevada. 0:55

— PAGE 52

7
LARRY SCHUTTE: Oasis, Nevada. "Nighttime in Nevada" (traditional). A romantic song from one-horse casinos on the Nevada desert. Learned from a scratchy old record by the legendary Sons of the Pioneers singers. Recorded by Hal Cannon, April 1993. 2:46

— PAGE 62

8
LINDA HASSELSTROM: Hermosa, South Dakota. "Carolyn, Miranda, and Me." From her book *Land Circle: Writings Collected from the Land* (1992). The skewed events and conversations of this poem create a sharply focused image of everyday life on a ranch. Recorded by Linda Hasselstrom, April 1993. 2:43

— PAGE 66

9

ROD McQUEARY: Ruby Valley, Nevada. "For Souls" and "For Life." Cowboys are not isolated from the world. Rod is also a Vietnam veteran, a philosopher, and a lyrical poet, which can be heard in these recent works. Recorded at the 1993 Cowboy Poetry Gathering, Elko, Nevada. *3:47*

—PAGE 72

10

J. B. ALLEN: Whiteface, Texas. "Rites of Passage" and "I'd Like to Be in Texas for the Roundup in the Spring" (Anonymous). A rite of passage on a cattle roundup, written by J.B., is followed by an all-time cowboy favorite, a nostalgic view of what the reciter calls the "almost mystical affinity Texans have for their home range." Recorded at the 1993 Cowboy Poetry Gathering, Elko, Nevada. *5:05*

—PAGE 80

11

R. W. HAMPTON: Stead, New Mexico. "Donny Catch a Horse for Me." Backed up by the musicians of Everywhere West and Lanny Fiel, R.W. sings a song of yearning for the good horse, the good ride, the good woman, and some fair scenery. Recorded at the 1993 Cowboy Poetry Gathering, Elko, Nevada. *4:55*

—PAGE 84

12

PAUL ZARZYSKI: Augusta, Montana. "The Roughstockaholic's 'Just-One-More-Last-One' Blues." Paul has tried for many years to give up riding rodeo . . . . Jack Stanton is a famous Australian rodeo or buckjump champ. Recorded at the 1993 Cowboy Poetry Gathering, Elko, Nevada. *4:31*

—PAGE 90

13

WALLACE McRAE: Forsyth, Montana. "Reincarnation." This may be the most famous contemporary cowboy poem, now recited all over the West. Recorded at the 1993 Cowboy Poetry Gathering, Elko, Nevada. *2:05*

—PAGE 96

14

IAN TYSON: High River, Alberta, Canada. "Cowboy Pride." This is one of the songs Ian wrote in a cabin in the Rocky Mountain foothills in 1985 for his album *Cowboyography*. *3:34*

—PAGE 104

15

WADDIE MITCHELL: Elko, Nevada. "Where to Go." A recent poem by Waddie from his 1993 Warner Western Records album, *Buckaroo Poet*. *3:43*

—PAGE 110

16

DON EDWARDS: Weatherford, Texas. "Colorado Trail" (traditional) from his Warner Western Records album *Songs of the Trail* (1992). First transcribed by a doctor who heard his cowboy patient singing it in a Duluth, Minnesota, hospital bed, this song is for Don one of the most beautiful cowboy ballads ever written. *2:57*

—PAGE 116

17

RIDERS IN THE SKY. The Nashville-based trio, accompanied by Don Edwards, sing the classic Western song "Home on the Range" at the final Ranch Family Matinee of the 1992 Cowboy Poetry Gathering in Elko, Nevada. The most recent album by Riders in the Sky, *Merry Christmas from Harmony Ranch,* appeared with Columbia Records in 1992. *4:15*

Total playing time: *59:32.* ADD and DDD

Further Listening and Reading

For the most complete listing of publications about the American cowboy, contact the Western Folklife Center, P.O. Box 888, Elko, Nevada, or phone 1-800-748-4466. The Western Folklife Center is a non-profit institution dedicated to the authentic folk arts of the American West. The WFC sponsors the Cowboy Poetry Gathering which is held every year during the last week of January.

The Bunkhouse Orchestra: *Old-Time Cowboy Songs,* book/cassette, ed. Hal Cannon. Gibbs Smith, Publisher
Don Edwards: *Songs of the Trail* and *Goin' Back to Texas.* Warner Western Records
R.W. Hampton: *The One I Never Could Ride.* Adobe Records
Waddie Mitchell: *Buckaroo Poet* and *Lone Driftin' Rider.* Warner Western Records
Michael Martin Murphy: *Cowboy Songs.* Warner Bros. Records
Buck Ramsey: *Rolling Uphill from Texas.* Fiel Publications, Inc.
Sons of the San Joaquin: *Songs of the Silver Screen* and *A Cowboy Has to Sing.* Warner Western Records
Red Steagall: *Born to This Land.* Warner Western Records; *Cowboy Favorites.* RS Records
Ian Tyson: *Cowboyography, I Outgrew the Wagon, And Stood There Amazed,* and *Old Corrals and Sagebrush and Other Cowboy Culture Classics.* Vanguard Records (USA), Stony Plain Records (Canada)

Back in the Saddle Again, American Cowboy Songs. New World Records
The Best of the Cowboy Poetry Gathering. Rhino Records
Cowboy Songs on Folkways. Smithsonian/Folkways
Songs of the West. 4 CD set, Rhino Records

NOTES ON OTHER CONTRIBUTORS

WILLIAM ALBERT ALLARD has been published in *National Geographic* magazine for thirty years. He is well known for his work on the American cowboy and has published three books, among them *Vanishing Breed* (1982), which was nominated for the American Book Award and was cited by the National Cowboy Hall of Fame as the year's outstanding Western art book. He lives near Charlottesville, Virginia.

HAL CANNON, advisor and audio editor for *Buckaroo*, is the founding director of the Cowboy Poetry Gathering in Elko, Nevada, an event credited with nurturing the renaissance of cowboy poetry and music. He has edited seven books on folk arts of the West, including two popular anthologies of verse, *Cowboy Poetry* and *New Cowboy Poetry: A Contemporary Gathering*. He is an accomplished musician and lives with his wife Teresa Jordan in Starr Valley, Nevada.

PETER DE LORY's work has been featured in museum exhibitions across the country. He received a Photography Fellowship from the National Endowment for the Arts in 1979 and an Artist Fellowship from the California Council in 1990. His book *The Wild and the Innocent* was published in 1987. He lives in San Francisco, California.

JAY DUSARD received a Guggenheim fellowship in photography in 1981 which led to the book, *The North American Cowboy: A Portrait*, published in 1983. One of America's best-known Western photographers, he has worked as a cowboy and has lived in Prescott, Arizona, for the past thirty years.

BANK LANGMORE covered more than twenty thousand miles, much of it on horseback, during the 1970s as he rode and worked with vaqueros, cowboys and buckaroos, from Mexico to Montana, making more than fifteen thousand exposures recording the contemporary working cowboy. He lives in San Antonio, Texas.

KURT MARKUS's best known books are *After Barbed Wire* (1985) and *Buckaroo* (1987). One of today's top fashion photographers, Kurt still keeps his hand in the cowboy world and is preparing a picture book about the cowboys of the southwest United States. He lives in Montana.

WILLIAM MATTHEWS was creative director and watercolor artist for this book. He lives in Evergreen, Colorado, and shows his works at The William Matthews Gallery in Denver. Much praised for the fresh style he has brought to Western painting, he is completing a forthcoming volume of his own work, *Cowboys and Images*, which will be published by Callaway Editions in 1994.

NORMAN MAUSKOPF has published two books of his photography, *Rodeo* in 1985 and *Dark Horses* in 1988, and is working on a new picture project dealing with the Mississippi Delta. He is based in Santa Fe, New Mexico.

MARTIN SCHREIBER spent more than a year riding with cowboys from the Oklahoma-Texas-New Mexico area, documenting life on a dozen ranches for his book, *The Last of a Breed*, published in 1982. Known also for his fashion and portrait photography, Schreiber now lives in France.

THOMAS WEST, the editor of *Buckaroo*, is a playwright and author of several books on literature, including *Ted Hughes*, a study of the British Poet Laureate. The former chief editor of the magazine *Art International* and a frequent contributor on BBC radio, he co-edited the book *Two Lives, Georgia O'Keeffe & Alfred Stieglitz* for Callaway Editions/HarperCollins in 1992.

ACKNOWLEDGMENTS

The concept of this book originated with Peter de Lory, who took the majority of portraits of the cowboy poets and musicians. Many thanks, pard.

Thanks to the Western Folklife Center for making available recordings from the Cowboy Poetry Gathering. Cowboy Poetry Gathering recordings were made by Performance Audio. Audio mix by Klay Anderson Audio, Ken Kruckenberg, and Richard Burton. Further mixing by Harmonic Ranch, New York.

Thanks to Warner Western Records for support and encouragement throughout this project.

Special thanks to Ralph Lauren for permission to use Kurt Markus's photograph of wild horses on pages 2-3 from Mr. Lauren's Double RL brand advertising campaign.

Warm thanks to all the writers and musicians who traveled the extra mile with us in trying to make a book that did justice to the great tradition of cowboy poetry and music. Thanks buckaroos and buckarettes!

Grateful acknowledgment is given for use of copyright material:

To the estate of S. Omar Barker for permission to reprint "Cowpen Moo-sic." To the estate of Charles Badger Clark for permission to reprint "The Old Cow Man." To the estate of Curley Fletcher for permission to reprint "The Sheep-herder's Lament." To the estate of Bruce Kiskaddon for permission to reprint "That Little Blue Roan," "When They've Finished Shipping Cattle in the Fall," "Alone," and "The Old Night Hawk." To Pantheon Books, New York, New York, for permission to reprint "Kelley" from *Riding the White Horse Home* by Teresa Jordan. To Fulcrum Publishing, Golden, Colorado, for permission to publish a sound recording of the poem "Carolyn, Miranda, and Me" from *Land Circle: Writings Collected from the Land* by Linda Hasselstrom. To Texas Tech University Press for permission to reprint "Anthem" from *As I Rode Out on the Morning* by Buck Ramsey. To Vanguard Records for permission to produce under license the track "Cowboy Pride" (music and lyrics by Ian Tyson ASCAP/Slick Fork Music CAPAC) from *Cowboyography*. To Warner Bros. Records, Inc., for permission to produce under license the track "Colorado Trail" (public domain, arranged by Don Edwards, Night Horse Songs BMI) from *Songs of the Trail*, Ⓟ 1992. To Warner Bros. Records Inc. for permission to produce under license the track "Where to Go" (poem by Waddie Mitchell; music by Joey Miskulin and David Hoffner, All Over Town Music/Sony Tree Publishing Co., Inc./Musicwagon Nashville/ Hoffner Haus BMI) from *Buckaroo Poet*, Ⓟ 1992. To Sony Tree Publishing Co. for permission to use "Where to Go" and "What Will I Tell Him" by Waddie Mitchell. To Fiel Publications, Inc. for permission to use the track "Git Along Little Dogies" (public domain, arranged by Buck Ramsey) from *Rolling Uphill from Texas*, Ⓟ 1992.

"Life and Times" by Rod McQueary and "Ain't No Life after Rodeo" were first published by the *Dry Crik Review of Contemporary Cowboy Poetry*. "Old Anne" by Teresa Jordan was first published in *Northern Lights*.

Collector Credits: Thanks are given to collectors for permission to reprint the following works by William Matthews: *Montana*, p. 1, Patricia Calhoun; *Hogback Orchard*, p. 24, private collection; *Repose*, p. 27, James G. Hansen; *Currycomb*, p. 75, Martha L. Bennett; *Heading Up to French Glen*, p. 111, Mr. and Mrs. John Welisch; *Late in the Day*, p. 119, Mr. and Mrs. Brian McCoy. All other works are from the collection of William Matthews.

In some cases we have been unable to contact the copyright holders of certain material. An account remains open for them at the offices of Callaway Editions.

OVERLEAF: Buckaroo Saddle, photograph by Bank Langmore

Buckaroo, Visions and Voices of the American Cowboy was produced by Callaway Editions:
Nicholas Callaway, Editorial Director, Charles Melcher, Publisher.

Creative Director: William Matthews.
Designer: Toshiya Masuda, assisted by
Kyoko Tateno, Masayo Hirano, and José Rodríguez.
Black and white film maker: Thomas Palmer, Newport, Rhode Island.
Color film maker: Universal Press, Providence, Rhode Island.

Production Director: True Sims, assisted by Ivan Wong, Jr.

Editorial assistance by Antoinette White,
Meredith Ward, and Barbara Bergeron.

Publicity Director: Patti Richards.
Sales Associate: Anne Simmons.

General Administration: Monica Moran and Sophia Seidner.

Typesetting by Callaway Editions in Monotype Centaur, Adobe Trajan,
Bitstream Stuyvesant, and Monotype Engraver's Roman fonts.

Printed in five colors on 80 pound Consoweb Brillant Dull Text
by Universal Press, Providence, Rhode Island.

Printed in the United States of America.